DATE DUE

Return Material Promptly

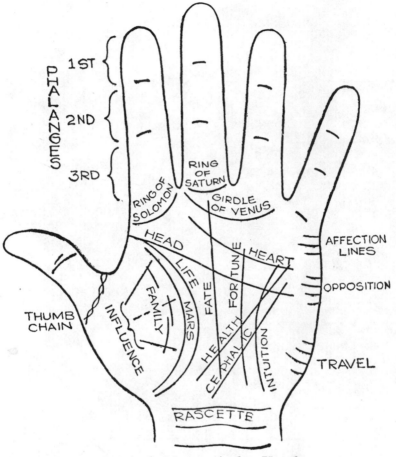

General Lines of the Hand

Litzka Raymond Gibson

HOW
TO
READ PALMS

Illustrated

FELL PUBLISHERS, INC.
Hollywood, Florida

Library of Congress Cataloging-in-Publications Data

Gibson, Litzka R.
  How to read palms.

   1. Palmistry. I. Title.
  BF921.G5   1989   133.6   88-83604
  ISBN 0-8119-0033-9

International Standard Business Number: 0-8119-0033-9
Library of Congress Card Catalog Number: 88-83604

For information address:

Fell Publishers, Inc.
2131 Hollywood Boulevard
Hollywood, Florida 33020

Published simultaneously in Canada by
Prentice-Hall Canada, Inc., Scarborough, Ontario

Manufactured in the United States of America
2 3 4 5 6 7 8 9 0

CONTENTS

Preface

PREFACE

I have often been asked how I became interested in palm analysis. I was in London, appearing as a concert harpist, and planning to return to America, when I met Maurice Raymond, the famous magician, whom I was to marry. He, too, was an American, and was known throughout the world as the Great Raymond. Then on a world tour, he needed specialty performers for the show. The tour intrigued me, so I signed with it.

The company went ahead to Portugal, where I was to join them. From Lisbon, Maurice cabled me to bring three new male assistants. I advertised in the newspapers, and from a wealth of applicants chose the three who most impressed me and had the most glowing letters of recommendation. I took them along to Portugal.

Before we finished our contracts in that country the three men that I had picked were all in jail. One was forging Maurice's checks, the second was caught robbing the box office, and the third tried to run away with a consul's daughter. I was naturally chagrined, but Maurice's only rebuke was this:

"Hereafter," he said, "instead of judging people by their appearance, personality, and wonderful letters of recommendation, you should study their palms and from them learn to read their real character."

I thought at first that he was joking, but he told me that throughout the world he had run into many instances where the language of the palm proved universal. He was familiar with the rudiments of palmistry but had never found time for its further study. Since I was not pressed for time, he suggested that I apply myself to the subject.

That I did, and I have never regretted it. From what I learned from books I literally opened a world of opportunities. During four world tours with the Great Raymond show I not only was able to compare the actual palms of nearly every race, civilized or savage, I also met students of palmistry in many lands and discussed their findings with them.

You, too, can learn from books as I have. In this book I have defined the groundwork of palm analysis and carried it through progressive stages, so that it forms a complete but compact guide. It is through the reading of palms themselves that you will gain the fine points of the subject. Yet the further you go the more valuable will the book become in telling what to look for and interpreting what is found.

Palmistry is not a "gift," as some people claim. Nothing of the mystic or the occult governed my own approach to the subject. Indeed, as the wife of a great magician, I often helped debunk the so-called psychic. Whether palm analysis should be rated as a science is something else that is useless to debate.

I have found palmistry to be more a language, which the palm itself speaks, or at least expresses. Treated as such, this book provides the syntax, grammar, and vocabulary. The interpretation of that language is yours from here on, and the further you progress in it, the more you will agree with me.

HOW
TO
READ PALMS

CHAPTER 1

THE STUDY OF THE PALM

As a natural preliminary to the study of the palm observations must be made of the hand as a whole. Even at a distance—or a glance—hands often give clues to a person's traits. When examined more closely, they reveal further details, so many, indeed, that the analysis of the hand may be regarded as a science in itself.

In a survey of the hand, the fingers are included as component parts of the hand itself and they are checked for further findings. Next, the analysis carries to the thumb, which may be termed the governor of the entire hand. Here the comparison of a person's two hands becomes of vital importance. What one thumb lacks, the other may supply.

This rule is true of the hands in their entirety, but it becomes strongly apparent with the thumbs and even more so as we proceed to a study of the palms themselves. Hence it is important to define the hands according to their individual influences.

The left palm of a right-handed person should be studied first. It is the *subjective* palm, representing a fundamental design which a person would naturally yearn to follow. Primitive persons or those who lead an untrammeled or sheltered life might be guided almost entirely by the influences of the subjective palm. This is probably why some of the early analysts recommended its reading alone as necessary.

The right is the *objective* palm, showing inclinations which a person may develop or follow, either under circumstance or stress. Its activities may evidence themselves through necessity or because of a broader—though not always wiser—outlook upon life. The objective palm may show a change of course pointing to ruin or success through the abandonment of a natural bent. Or, where large or serious issues do not enter a person's life, the interpretations of the objective palm may simply represent reluctance toward following the paths that the subjective palm portrays.

Catch phrases applied to the palms: "The left shows what you have and the right shows what you may make of it" are good as far as they go. The real interpretations, however, lie deeper. The subjective palm shows inclinations much of a hereditary nature, while the objective discloses a person's reactions to environment. The erroneous notion that one hand tells the "past" and the other the "future" dates back to the still-more-discredited idea that "fortunes" can be told from the palm. There is nothing of such humbug or pretended occultism in character reading through scientific palm analysis.

The readings are reversed with a left-handed person. The right palm becomes the subjective; the left, the objective. The rules of natural bent for the subjective and applied effort for the objective are used accordingly.

The palm itself is divided into nine areas, eight of which are termed "mounts" because they often show a pronounced cushion or rise. These areas have been named after various planets, which, through tradition, are representative of certain qualities, namely: Ambition, wisdom, talent, discernment, imagination, sympathy, and forcefulness.

Thus the study of the mounts becomes a fascinating subject in itself and forms the background for the further reading of the palm. A well-developed mount shows the presence of its trait, but when overdeveloped good qualities

. are dissipated. Ambition may become arrogance, wisdom may turn into melancholy. Absence of a mount is not always a negative token; sometimes it produces traits of their own individual form.

Upon these areas which represent life purposes are etched various lines and lesser markings that activate the qualities of the mounts. Minor markings may be regarded as features of the mounts themselves, strengthening or weakening them. The stronger lines, termed the general lines of the palm, are the stamp of individual behavior as well as personality.

These are not mere creases formed by opening and closing the hand. They are so fundamentally a feature of the palm itself that they persistently retain their courses against the influx of other folds. As all persons differ in moods and traits, so do these lines follow paths of their own, like outward engravings that symbolize the inner being. When studied in such light, remarkable accuracy has been gained in their interpretations as with other features also resident upon the palm.

On most palms three basic lines attract immediate notice. One is the Line of Life, curving around the base of the thumb. The next is the Line of Head, crossing the palm just above the center. The third is the Line of Heart, which lies farther above, curving downward from the base of the fingers. All these are subject to considerable variation; therein they represent a personal story. They show the mental and physical capacities of the individual as applied to his existing traits.

Among the secondary lines are those of Fate, Fortune, and Health, styled Lines of Destiny. They represent pathways which may be followed and the extent to which abilities may be applied or used. Such lines appear upon most palms, or can at least be partially traced there. Along with a few other secondaries are numerous lesser lines, some quite rare but all subject to special interpretations. These form the final etchings in the pattern of the palm. Often such lesser lines or minor markings provide the minute details that add the high lights of the finished story.

As we have traced it, the study of the palm definitely follows a course from the general to the specific, beginning with the hand as a whole and ending in specialized details. How the findings should be weighed and balanced is something that will be learned through practice and experience.

Where indications are plain or decidedly emphatic, they should be regarded as strong points in a reading. When doubtful, they should be checked for corroboration elsewhere. Always remember that the comparison of one hand with the other may clarify many points, often producing balance rather than conflict. This becomes progressively apparent as a reading proceeds from the hand in general to the lines in particular.

Having set the formula for a hand and palm analysis, the chapters in this book will follow the rotation as given. As a preliminary, however, we are inserting a brief key chapter which will serve both as a supplement to the present introduction and a guide to the material which forms the body of the volume.

CHAPTER 2

HOW TO READ A PALM

This chapter serves as a key to the progressive steps in palm analysis. Any technical or unfamiliar terms are amplified by giving the numbers of the chapters in which they are detailed. Once those chapters have been studied, all statements given here will not only be understandable, they will serve as reference in the course of a palm reading.

For convenience the progress of a reading has been divided into twelve steps, as follows:

1. Type the hand and fingers according to their shape, classing them as pointed, conical, spatulate, square, or mixed. This will tell whether a person's over-all approach to life is idealistic, inspirational, energetic, orderly, or adaptable. (Chapter 3.)

2. Check the hand for consistency and flexibility. Note the thumb angle. Check finger joints as smooth or knotty. Add any indications from the fingernails.

3. Class the fingers as long, showing love of detail; or short, signifying impatience. Note any variance of finger types or phalanges. Check these findings with each separate finger to judge their individual attributes. (Chapter 4.)

4. Note slant and set of fingers along with any minor features that may tally with major findings. These slight indications are often valuable in judging other traits.

5. Analyze the thumb and its set. Note its length and

check same by type. Study the thumb phalanges. For further findings check shape, flexibility, consistency, and nails. Here a comparison of thumbs for subjective and objective is important and the same rule of comparison must be remembered during all the steps that follow. (Chapter 5.)

6. Study the palm areas. Check each for traits as indicated by development, overdevelopment, or absence of mounts. Remember that each has a bearing upon a person's composite character. (Chapter 6.)

7. Continue with more detailed study of the developed mounts. Add or subtract the values of the markings that appear upon them. Check the fingers for values in relation to the mounts. Thus determine the strongest mount (or mounts) along with any unusual features. (Chapter 7.)

8. Build the readings through the combinations of the more important mounts, as determined in the previous step. Study their blends or conflicts as described in the various charts. Check these for strength or weakness by data already gained. (Chapter 8.)

9. Study the basic Lines of Life, Head, and Heart. Consider their points of origin, extent, and other general indications. Check any breaks or markings on one line against those of the others. This means using the Time Chart (Chapter 10) in connection with the summary of the basic lines. (Chapter 11.) Set aside any doubtful findings until later in the analysis. During the study of the three basic lines, note any strong secondary lines and begin to tally them on the Time Chart so they can be checked against the basic lines.

10. Begin an analysis of the Destiny Lines, if any appear. Should they appear strongly, they will already have come in for some consideration. Both as strengtheners and checks on time periods, there is a relation between these lines and those of Life, Head, and Heart. This applies in particular to the Line of Life and the Line of Health, which have an unusual relation. Add findings from any other secondary lines. (Chapter 12.)

11. After rounding out the analysis, look for specific details among the lesser lines (Chapter 13) and check any odd markings so far overlooked. (Chapter 14.) Here you may find some very unusual signs or indications. Often these add a surprise element to the palm. Remember also that lines can change and that they may be repaired or impaired as time goes on.

12. Add the evidence gained. Any important findings should be corroborated elsewhere on the palm in order to become high lights. These constitute the main features of the reading, with the other facts to fill the story.

You will find that the twelve steps as here given have been followed in the specimen palm reading that appears in Chapter 15, where you will also note a comparison of two palms (subjective and objective). One final point should be stressed, however, in concluding this key chapter.

The point is this: More and more, as you proceed with palm readings, you will discover the remarkable individualities that appear upon the palms of different persons. Each tells its own story and therefore constitutes a book in itself. Do not expect the features of palms to conform to any set of rules. The descriptions given in the following chapters are simply the norms by which variants can be gauged.

Hence some striking departure from the conventional markings of a palm is often to be expected and is worthy of an individualistic interpretation more than a freakish one. Keeping your twelve steps in mind, check them against the factors that they represent, and with each succeeding palm reading you will find yourself more skilled in your final appraisal.

CHAPTER 3

A SURVEY OF THE HAND

The first survey of the hand should be made from the back. Also, both hands should be studied to learn whether they conform in pattern or to detect any marked differences. Both hands should be placed flat on the table or upon the analyst's own palms. Thus the hands can be compared and classified first according to certain types.

These types are judged by their shape, not only that of the hand proper but of the thumb and fingers. It is seldom that hands are of "pure" types, but if the thumb and fingers all conform to one specification, a hand may be classed in that type, unless the hand proper is at total variance.

For practical purposes, even a slight deviation of one or two fingers is allowable when typing the hand as a whole. In palmistry the thumb and various fingers have strong individual interpretations, hence will be separately typed when their own cases come up for consideration.

So this preliminary survey is at most a generalization where a person's characteristics are concerned. A "pure" type can be sharply classified, but for the most part a fair appraisal of the individual's natural bent is all that can be expected this early in the analysis. However, the shapes of the thumb and fingers should be carefully checked for later tabulation where their types are separately studied.

POINTED　　　CONICAL

SPATULATE　　　SQUARE

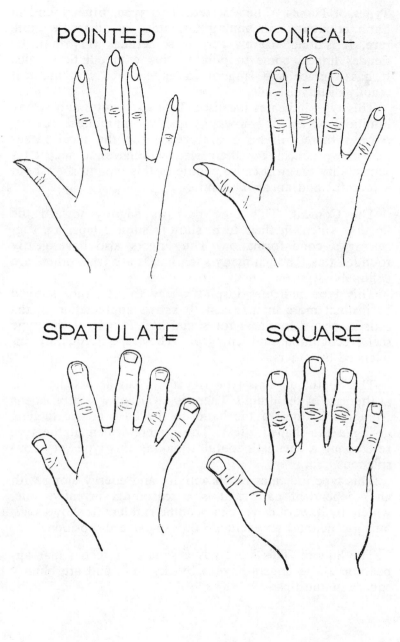

Types of Hands The Pointed. This type, often found in Latin countries and among Orientals, is otherwise quite rare. It is long, narrow across, sometimes very thin. Its slender fingers come to pointed tips with elliptical nails. It has a grace and languor in appearance that make it readily distinguishable.

This type indicates idealism, love of beauty, and strong intuition. Often it shows a highly impractical nature. Always there will be a preference for the ideal rather than the practical, but there is a willingness to accept responsibility that will cause people of this type to show both a forceful and an abiding side.

The Conical. This type narrows slightly toward the fingers, which, in their turn, show a similar tapering, suggesting a cone formation. The fingers also have gently rounded tips. Though many such hands are frail, others are definitely of strong, heavy formation.

This type indicates inspiration, with a nature swayed by instinct more than reason. It shows appreciation of the artistic, also a fondness for social life. People of this type seek recognition and enjoy it. They are frequently influenced by others.

The Spatulate. This type is very broad across the hand at the base of the thumb. There is a variant which broadens from the bottom of the hand to the base of the fingers, giving a fan-shaped effect. The fingers widen at the top, resembling a chemist's spatula, making this type very conspicuous.

This type indicates much activity and energy along with an independent nature. It is a reasoning, inventive one, which, by its very drive, can become ruthless. It shows skill, but also denotes an excitable or explosive disposition.

The Square. This hand has a square or rectangular appearance. The fingers have a blocky look and are bluntly square at the tips.

This type shows a practical nature with a desire for order and system. It represents a steady, plodding disposition, with an acceptance of custom and conditions. Such people, however, can be strongly set in their opinions. Forceful, they can prove successful even though confining themselves to narrow interests.

The Mixed. This is a composite of the various types, which can sometimes be reduced to a combination of two, showing the traits of both, often in sharp contrast. Generally speaking, it represents adaptability because of its make-up. This may produce a versatile individual, with many unusual flairs. There is, however, the presence of uncertainty, which leads to fear of failure.

Never so easy to interpret as the "pure" types, the mixed type is nevertheless most frequently seen among North Americans. With such a hand the type of thumb is often its predominating factor and may therefore be used as a basis of interpretation.

From the type is gained a general impression of a person's underlying nature. There is a hand called the Elemental Type, thick, wide, clumsy, and with a short-thumbed formation seldom seen among civilized peoples. It represents primitive and often brutal traits.

In contrast, long, bony, expressive hands with knotty joints on thumb and fingers have been termed the Philosophical Type, indicating silent, deep thinkers, whose chief quest is wisdom. This, however, is largely a traditional classification denoting an unusually knotty hand, inasmuch as hands of the basic types often have fingers with knotted joints, and therefore include many of the so-called philosophicals.

Flexibility of Hands Hands may be tested for flexibility by gently bending them backward from the tips of the fingers. These fall into three categories:

Stiff. These, when open, show an inward curve and

refuse to bend backward to any appreciable degree. People with these hands are usually watchful and hard to convince. They often seek proof before trusting their own judgment. Once decided, they stay firm. They have a strongly reliable tendency.

Pliable. These are the sort which bend back rather noticeably but not to an extreme. People with this type vary, some having hands which are almost straight, others quite pliant. They are often easy to deal with, taking the usual run of things in a reasonable way.

Extremely pliable. These are hands which bend far backward, sometimes to a remarkable degree. They represent people with extreme natures. They tend toward Bohemian tastes and frequently have many interests and abilities.

Note: Sometimes one person's hands vary in flexibility, showing a balance of trends, though with age a person with differing hands is apt to be variable, swinging from one to the other.

Consistency of Hands In testing hands for flexibility, the analyst, in feeling the hand, can begin to note its consistency. This is done by touch rather than observation. By pressing a hand from beneath and above, kneading it slightly from various angles, you can ascertain whether it is any one of the following:

Hard. This is a hand which is definitely unyielding, the flesh almost stiff to the touch. It is the resolute hand, strong in nature and with an emphasis on the physical.

Firm. Sometimes termed "elastic," this hand has a definite give, somewhat springy to the touch. It shows a spirited nature, usually with pronounced determination. People with this type are equipped to accept life's contrasts and meet its conflicts.

Soft. Such a hand lacks resistance when pressed, giving a limp impression to the touch. It indicates a love of luxury, a dislike for drudgery. The soft hand should not be underestimated. Some of the world's most clever and brilliant people possess such hands.

Flabby. Noticeably loose and puffy, this hand denotes tendencies to excesses and indolence. It shows a variance of disposition, ranging from geniality to temper. Discounting any glandular condition, the character represented by the flabby hand depends upon the signs of the palm for strengthening forces.

Note: Sometimes a person's hands vary in consistency and therefore must be considered a blend or conflict of two classifications. The exact status can be determined by corroborative evidence in the reading of the palm.

Having tested the consistency of the hand, the next simple and logical step is to learn the thumb angle.

The Thumb Angle Placing the hands flat on the table, palms down, extend each thumb outward as far as it can go. This will show its angle of extension in relation to the hand. Should the limit be a narrow angle, with the thumb cramped close to the hand, it shows a cautious nature, sometimes selfish and rarely outspoken.

A wider spread, approaching the right angle but not reaching it will show forceful self-expression, dependent, of course, upon the person's other characteristics. But when the right angle is reached, it indicates an unmanageable nature that needs control. Beyond the right angle, persons are found whose behavior becomes quite unpredictable.

There is an increase of generosity or sentiment in the widening of this angle, but it passes the rational point as it nears the right angle and thereby defeats its purpose.

Much of a person's disposition depends upon the thumb. It shows the amount of will power and reasoning people exert over their affairs in life. Having determined the thumb angle, the thumb itself becomes a study which in regular practice can be conducted at this phase of the hand survey.

However, since the thumb will soon have a chapter to itself, it is now best to continue with the hand and fingers.

Following the hand upward, we reach the joints of the fingers.

The Finger Joints Smooth joints indicate spontaneous thought—a tendency to jump to conclusions. This is modified by the finger types. With pointed fingers, smooth joints —which usually occur—mark a person as almost completely intuitive.

Knotty joints have a definite, bony bulge, easily sensed by touch, often noticeable to the eye. They show analytical thought, desire for accuracy in detail. When highly pronounced on all the joints, they indicate a mind appreciating advanced logic, thus fitting the traditional term of "philosophical" hand.

Frequently the joints of a hand vary. The lower joints, when smooth, betoken quick thought in practical, everyday matters. When knotty, they show order in material things, with practical analysis. Smooth upper joints indicate quickness in ideas, even flashes of inspiration. Knotty upper joints show order in ideas, the desire to weigh decisions.

Time is needed in all important mental processes where knotty joints are concerned. Though the snap judgment of smooth-fingered persons may sometimes go wrong, those with knotty joints are often given credit for wisdom simply because they follow a habit of deliberation.

The Fingernails Short nails betoken a critical nature. Wide nails show an outspoken person, whether critical or not. Narrow nails indicate a guarded or secretive disposition. Curved nails, with a bulbous appearance, show jealousy. Fluted nails with lengthwise grooves indicate nervousness. Ridged nails with crosswise rises show irritability under stress. Tilted nails, the kind that bend upward or backward at the end, invariably show talent.

The fingernails are an index to minor characteristics that

could ordinarily be reserved for consideration until after a general analysis of the hand and palm. However, since they can be noted so conveniently during this first survey, it is good practice to do so. Often data gained from the fingernails will either corroborate or add side lights to more important information found upon the palm, and will thereby add to its interpretation.

Length of Fingers From the back of the hand note if the fingers, as a group, are approximately the same length as the hand proper. The measurement is made from the wrist to the knuckle of the second finger which, since it should normally be the longest finger, is taken as representative of the group. Hence that finger is in turn measured from the knuckle to the tip for comparison with the hand length. Those measurements should be approximately the same; otherwise, the hand will have:

Long fingers, which indicate a love of detail and therefore frequently show an inclination to worry over small things, often to the neglect of larger. Or

Short fingers, which show a quick nature, often amounting to impatience, plus a desire to consider a subject in its entirety and leave the details until later.

Note: These traits are also attributed to hands which are large or small in proportion to a person's size. But as the fingers display the same propensities, it is preferable to consider such characteristics in terms of long and short fingers, since in normal hands the fingers can then be gauged as individually long or short.

The Inside of the Hand When the hand is turned so that the palm is upward, it may be checked rapidly as to type: pointed, conical, spatulate, square, or mixed. The palm gives a better view for checking type than does the back of the hand. The shape of the fingers can again be noted to their tips, if only as a reminder.

There are many minor details regarding fingers, some

of which may frequently have an important bearing on a complete analysis of the palm. These will be discussed in a supplementary chapter. For the present there is one important feature that must be considered:

The Three Phalanges You will observe that the fingers are divided into three horizontal sections, each neatly marked off by crosslines. These are the phalanges: first, second, and third, which run in the order of higher, middle, and lower. Traditionally, these have been said to represent the "Three Worlds," from the philosophical idea of Soul, Mind, and Body. (See frontispiece.)

Such a variety of terms have been given to these three phalanges that should they be properly named it would still lead to confusion. Therefore, remembering that they are counted from the tip of the finger downward, it is preferable to define them simply as first, second, and third.

In a balanced hand the first phalanges are shorter than either the second or the third, the latter two being about equal in length. Thus, if the first phalanges have the approximate length of the others, individually, they are regarded as long phalanges; whereas the second or third, to be classed as long, would have to show a margin in actual measurement.

All three, in a sense, represent mental application. The first phalanges point toward intellectual accomplishment. The second phalanges indicate practical application. The third phalanges deal with material interests. Thus, in relation to the other two:

Long first phalanges show intellectual desire, the application of one's thoughts or capabilities to higher achievement.

Long second phalanges indicate the practical mind seeking constructive measures that can be applied to whatever is at hand, often in a commercial way.

Long third phalanges represent a mentality geared to material gain, valuing only whatever can be turned to immediate use or profit.

Similarly, an unusually short phalange will show a lack of the quality represented. If all the fingers are uniform (where length of phalanges is concerned), it is possible to classify a person just as with "pure" finger types. But often the phalanges vary, just as do the fingers in the mixed type of hand.

This is no obstacle in the interpretation of the fingers. To the contrary, it furnishes all the more indications as to a person's inner traits. The rule to remember is this: Each finger should be evaluated both as to type and phalanges, along with other features, which can be ascertained by comparing the fingers.

This leads to a study of the individual fingers and will require a brief chapter in itself. Since each finger has an interpretation in terms of the palm, this carries the subject from hand analysis into palmistry proper. The fingers, as well as the thumb, which will have a chapter of its own, are the link between the two subjects.

Thus through observations on the individual fingers a preliminary treatment will be given to the subject of the palm, so that the reader will have more than an introductory knowledge of the interpretations to be discussed in later chapters.

Summary of Chapter 3

From the shape of a person's hands, including the thumb and fingers, you can type them as pointed, conical, spatulate, or square. These types, respectively, indicate idealism, inspiration, energy, and orderliness, though with certain oddities or extremes, as given. Where a type proves mixed, as is very common, you find an adaptable though sometimes confused personality.

With these types as a basis you can add further facts from a survey of the hand. Its flexibility is often reflected in a person's nature. In consistency you will find hands hard, firm, soft, and flabby. These are keys to a resolute nature, determination, love of luxury, and indolence, in the order named.

The thumb angle, namely the spread of the thumb from beside the hand, shows you everything from a cautious, selfish nature to an unmanageable or unpredictable temperament, according to the angle's increasing width.

From the finger joints you can determine persons who are spontaneous in thought or those of analytical minds, according to whether the joints are smooth or knotty. As minor indexes to character, even the fingernails give you the following data: short, a critical nature; wide, outspoken; narrow, secretive; curved, jealous; fluted, nervous; ridged, irritable; tilted, talented.

Long fingers show love of detail; short fingers, impatience. With these your survey includes the length of the three phalanges. The first (higher) is intellectual; the second (middle) is practical; the third (lower) is material. These qualities are emphasized by an unusual length of any phalange.

CHAPTER 4

THE INDIVIDUAL FINGERS

In palmistry, the four fingers have been named according to the palm areas at their bases. This nomenclature will be followed because it is convenient and consistent. Also, by considering the fingers in those terms, the reader will find himself familiar with them when he studies the palm areas, or mounts.

Counting from the index finger, the fingers are named as follows: 1, Finger of Jupiter; 2, Finger of Saturn; 3, Finger of Apollo; 4, Finger of Mercury.

The qualities attributed to those fingers, because of the respective palm areas beneath them, are: 1, Jupiter—ambition; 2, Saturn—wisdom; 3, Apollo—talent; 4, Mercury—discernment.

Each finger type influences those individual traits. Thus if the fingers are all of the pointed type, a person will show ideals in ambition, knowledge, artistry, and business. Conical fingers will apply an inspirational touch to those qualities. Spatulate fingers show energy and independence. The square type reveal a practical, orderly mind where those traits are concerned.

In the analysis of a mixed hand the fingers must be considered separately. Often this will show peculiar blends or conflicts in a person's nature.

For instance, a person with a Jupiter Finger of the conical type and a Mercury Finger of the spatulate type would have unusual ambitions, plus the constant desire to push them to a rapid and profitable conclusion.

Other combinations offer keys to individual character, but in themselves the finger types are simply guides to further interpretations. They represent a person's approach to life, or in many cases its acceptance. The question of good or bad, help or hindrance, depends on what else the fingers show; and the fingers, in turn, must be considered in relation to the palm areas.

As an example: A person with a Jupiter Finger of the square type would normally further an ambition in a practical way. The question is whether that person would be ambitious in the first place, and, if so, on how great a scale. His life might be strictly commonplace, with no purposes to be furthered through practical treatment.

Once finger types are studied, it is intriguing to observe how people conform to them in small or casual matters. Indeed, fingers have been treated as a subject in themselves, and the same applies to the thumb. Hence, here we can delve into the finer phases of finger analysis, gaining data that can later be checked against the findings from the palm.

With each finger the three sections or phalanges should be considered individually. These show a person's application of the intellectual, the practical, and the material, as defined in the previous chapter. Here are a variety of intriguing prospects.

A long first phalange of Saturn combined with a long second phalange of the Mercury Finger indicates scholarly interests plus a direct business sense. This combination might be found on the fingers of a successful encyclopedia salesman. Many similar examples may be found through a study of the phalanges.

Knotty joints show an analytical mind. Smooth joints show spontaneous thought. Since the joints link the phalanges, they connect the intellectual, practical, and material spheres. Thus a knotty upper joint indicates order in ideas, a reluctance to accept the new. Such joints show persons who are often doubters. A smooth upper joint shows a person who sparks ideas and often has spurts of inspiration.

A knotty lower joint shows order in material things. It is a calculating token, marking the person who thinks everything out, weighing its possible consequences. A smooth lower joint shows quick thought along such channels; no time wasted in debate or considering of minor, detailed phases.

These rules apply to the individual fingers. Knotty joints with Jupiter indicate careful calculation toward ambition; smooth knots mark the opportunist. Knotty joints with Saturn show a profound thinker; smooth joints, the person who gathers knowledge quickly though often not so thoroughly.

A knotted Apollo Finger portrays a person who will study to develop his talents and may be meticulous in many things. Smooth joints indicate people who grasp things easily. Knots with the Mercury Finger show a person who puts system into enterprise; smooth joints indicate people who make quick business decisions.

Knots are extremely rare on fingers of the pointed type. A knot on a conical finger is usually slight but can be detected by pressing the sides of the joint lightly between a thumb and forefinger, which may then be moved up and down along the finger. Knots are quite common on fingers of the spatulate and square types and must be readily discernible to be regarded as active on fingers of those types.

When the palm areas are discussed in a later chapter, the influence of finger types will be given also, both in positive and negative aspects. Then the full importance of the pointed, conical, spatulate, and square finger will be understandable in terms of ambition, wisdom, talent, and discernment, as well as other traits.

There are other features of the individual fingers, however, that should be considered here, as they show some relationship between the fingers themselves. Their importance, however, will be all the more amplified in terms of the palm areas; therefore, the reader should study their details now, and remember to check back. The features to be discussed may strengthen or weaken the significance of a palm area, thus playing a vital part in its interpretation.

Length of Individual Fingers It has been stated that the normal length of the fingers, as a group, is equal to that of the hand proper, when viewed from the back, with the knuckle of the Saturn Finger as a mid-point between the tip of that finger and the wrist. In comparing the lengths of the fingers individually, it is preferable to study them from the inside of the hand. Assuming that the Saturn Finger is approximately of normal length, the following measurements will conform to the same standard:

The Jupiter and Apollo Fingers should be equal in length, each extending to the middle of the first phalange of the Saturn Finger. The Mercury Finger should reach to the upper joint of the Apollo Finger.

It is from these measurements—whether actual or imaginary—that each individual finger may be gauged as long or short. In some hands the Saturn Finger itself is either long or short. In such cases, if the other fingers conform to the usual proportions, they accordingly would be regarded as long or short. In brief, the Saturn Finger is merely taken as a common denominator, not as an actual yardstick.

With a long Saturn Finger (first measured from the back of the hand) it is easy to check what the normal length of that finger should be and thus class each of the remaining fingers as long or short, except, of course, when they are approximately normal. A similar check may be made by adding a slight imaginary length to a short Saturn Finger. With the remaining fingers, any long finger may make the one adjoining it appear short, but by keeping the normal measurements in mind, there is no trouble in defining them.

When a finger goes appreciably beyond its normal extent, it is considered long, and the farther it extends, the more extreme its tendencies will be. When a finger becomes very long, it is generally too extreme; this is often an unfavorable sign, though it may prove valuable when length is greatly needed in that particular finger to counterbalance a defect indicated somewhere else.

If the entire first phalange of the Saturn Finger should extend beyond normal length, as gauged by the distance from the wrist to the finger knuckle, the Saturn Finger would be regarded as very long. There are some hands in which all the fingers will show the same extreme lengths.

Based on a Saturn Finger of normal length, the other fingers will rate as very long if either the Jupiter or Apollo Finger extends to the tip of the Saturn Finger or beyond; or if the Mercury Finger goes higher than the mid-point of the first phalange of the Apollo Finger. These measurements, as mentioned earlier, are based on an approximation of the normal proportions.

When a finger falls below its normal measurement, it is regarded as short, and its tendencies increase in accordance with its shortness. A very short Saturn Finger would be almost the length of its first phalange below normal measurement. A very short Jupiter or Apollo Finger would not pass the upper joint of a normal Saturn Finger. A very short Mercury Finger would not come above the mid-point of the second phalange of a normal Apollo Finger.

All these measurements are somewhat approximate. In studying fingers it is easy to class them as long or short. When very long or very short, they are conspicuously out of proportion to any fingers that are approximately normal. When a hand is well proportioned, it should be given some benefit of doubt; that is, a hand with all fingers unusually long should not be charged off as very long and given unfavorable findings, for it has a balance of its own. It is when a finger is definitely long or short in relation to the others that it becomes a strong indication of certain characteristics or their lack.

A long finger indicates the presence of traits represented by that particular finger; a short finger shows their lack. Where the palm areas are well developed, as will be discussed later, a long finger strengthens any such area, while a short finger detracts from its qualities. Here, however, a very long finger adds too much to a developed area or mount, marking it as overdeveloped, which is unfavorable.

Lean and Set of Fingers Elaborate study could be made of individual fingers and their comparative lengths, but this would be of minor significance in relation to the more extensive facts to be gained from a reading of the palm areas themselves. However, the lean of the fingers shows a definite trend of one trait toward another, with somewhat unfavorable aspects.

Should the Jupiter Finger lean toward Saturn, ambition may be restricted to scholarly terms. Where the Saturn Finger leans toward Jupiter, it shows a morose nature, a handicap to ambition. A lean of the Saturn Finger toward Apollo is an exception to these unfavorable notes: it shows an application of a scholarly mind toward natural talents, often producing brilliance.

Where Apollo leans toward Saturn, vanity dominates personal accomplishment. A lean of Apollo toward Mercury shows a person who will sacrifice skill for money. A lean of the Mercury Finger toward the Apollo Finger, however, shows an ability to apply business judgment to natural gifts however much of either the person may possess.

Such leanings of the fingers are most noticeable toward the tips. There are cases where all the fingers show a general slant, either toward Jupiter or Mercury. In such instances a person will apply all his study, talent, or discernment toward ambition if the slant is toward the Jupiter

Finger. When toward the Mercury Finger, all ambition, knowledge or skill is applied to business or profit.

A crooked finger is either considerably bent sideways or shows a definite twist. It marks a wasteful streak in the field represented by that finger. With a long finger, it indicates irresponsibility; with a short finger, sheer indifference. It is a token of people who look out for their own interests but frequently defeat them. Strong lines of the palm are needed as a counterbalance.

The set of the fingers should be particularly noticed. With a square hand, the bases of the fingers are almost in a line; with others, they show a slight curve from one side of the hand to the other. Sometimes an individual finger, usually Jupiter or Mercury, is low set: that is, its base is noticeably below the normal line. Such a finger detracts seriously from the attributes of the mount it represents, often because it infringes upon the palm area itself. A low-set finger does not rate extra length: it is judged long or short by the extent of its tip, as with other fingers.

The spread of the fingers furnishes certain keys to character. The hand should be placed loosely but naturally on the table or on the analyst's own hand. If all the fingers spread apart, they show a person who cannot keep a secret. If the Finger of Jupiter extends somewhat straight but the others curl, it shows a constant demand for leadership, conscious or unconscious; always, among a group of people, a person with that extended finger will try to hold the floor.

A spread between the Fingers of Jupiter and Saturn stands for independence of thought; between Saturn and Apollo, a careless or carefree disposition; between Apollo and Mercury, independence of action. Sometimes two of these are seen in combination and have the dual interpretation. All fingers kept close together indicates a secretive and sometimes fearful disposition. These points can often be noted when a hand is in action, allowing preliminary findings prior to a palm analysis.

Other Finger Features High cushions, that is, noticeable pads on the first phalanges, denote great sensitivity, particularly applicable to the traits of any fingers on which they are prominent. People with these traits are not always touchy but will almost always appreciate the sentiments of others.

A thin finger shows a delicacy of nature; a thick finger indicates a practical or self-indulgent trend. Where the third phalanges taper almost to a waist at the base, they signify curiosity. This is applicable to the fingers as a group; but when the third phalange of any finger is thick, almost barrel-shaped in contrast to the other phalanges, it shows an extremist in material ways toward whatever matters that finger symbolizes. If the third phalange is long, such moods will be dominant, but often the thickness is found when the third phalange is short. It still means, however, that the person will want to see material results from ambition, study, talent, or business. This has a practical side, but beneath it is a selfish trend that may thwart a person's higher purposes, or create mistrust.

All these indications will be found useful after the palm areas have been studied, and should be checked against the findings there. They have been detailed in advance, because in analyzing a palm the customary procedure is to gain data from the fingers first, then check back as required.

Similarly, the thumb comes in for special study as a prelude to the interpretations of the palm, even more so than the fingers, as the thumb is a strongly governing force rather than a modifier. Hence the thumb will form the subject of the next chapter, completing the link between the surveys of the hand and the palm.

Summary of Chapter 4

Coming from a general survey to a specific study, you will find special keys to character emphasized by each finger. Beginning with the index finger, the fingers are named as follows, with their principal attributes: 1, Jupiter—ambition; 2, Saturn—wisdom; 3, Apollo—talent; 4, Mercury—discernment.

You will find features of the individual fingers covered in the foregoing chapter, partly as preliminary to the study of the palm. The type of each finger influences its traits, and from such study combinations of character are formed.

Long fingers show presence of desired traits, while short fingers indicate their lack. Very long fingers are often unfavorable, as they exaggerate certain traits. In connection with such data, methods of gauging and measuring the fingers are given, to determine their comparative lengths.

Even the slant of the fingers yields interpretations. Each finger that slants thus is influenced by the traits of the next, usually in an adverse way. A general lean toward Jupiter, however, shows an application chiefly to ambition; while a general lean toward Mercury shows a nature applied to business.

Crooked fingers show irresponsibility or indifference toward the qualities represented. Low-set fingers detract from such attributes. You will find that a person with spread fingers cannot keep a secret, while those who hold them close are sometimes fearful. Other indications are traced from finger spreads.

CHAPTER 5

THE STUDY OF THE THUMB

The analysis of character through a study of the thumb can be regarded as a subject in itself. Considering the hand in general, the thumb holds a strong sway over all the characteristics represented. In palmistry and its interpretations the thumb is the axis about which the other findings revolve.

As the art of palm reading emerged from mysticism, increased importance was given to the study of the thumb. It was largely from this fact that other features of the hand came under detailed observation, producing the science of hand analysis. Thus the thumb, as the basis of both branches of hand study, is also the link between them.

In discussing the individual fingers it was stated that their features are dependent upon the interpretation of the palm areas found below them. Therefore the fingers are of subordinate importance to those areas or mounts. With the thumb, the situation is practically reversed. At the base of the thumb is an area termed the Mount of Venus. The major portion of this area is composed of the third phalange or lower portion of the thumb, which outwardly exhibits only two phalanges, the first and second.

Thus through a complete study of the thumb we find ourselves actually engaged in a reading of the palm, which could well be continued from that starting point, though in actual practice it is more convenient to take the mounts in rotation. Furthermore, since the Mount of Venus represents the emotional qualities found in a person's nature, its attributes—or lack of them—are reflected in the interpretations of all the other palm areas. Hence the thumb, controlling the Mount of Venus, is an index to a great variety of human traits.

The thumb, therefore, is indicative of a person's fundamental character. It shows the moral capacity of the individual. An entire reading of the palm can be "set" from the thumb; that is, as various traits are determined, their expression can be judged in terms of the thumb.

In discussion of the hand mention was made of the "thumb angle," which is ascertained when the hands are placed palms down upon the table and the thumbs extended to their limit. The width of this spread, as mentioned, indicates a person's degree of self-expression. This is restricted by a narrow angle; it becomes forceful with a wide angle; when it reaches the right angle it shows an unmanageable nature which may become unpredictable when the angle passes that degree.

Often, but not always, the thumb angle depends upon the position at which the thumb projects from the hand. The higher the set, the less the angle; the lower the set of the thumb, the greater the angle. This setting of the thumb is best studied by viewing the inside of the hand. It gives the following indications:

A high-set thumb shows a cautious nature with a stubborn tendency. A medium-set thumb is the sign of an adaptable person who avoids extremes. A low-set thumb indicates a careless nature with an overgenerous trend. These positions are gauged by a point about midway between the base of the fingers and the wrist.

Length of the Thumb The setting of the thumb must be observed, particularly from the inside of the hand, in order to gauge the length of the thumb, which is a very important indication. A medium-set thumb, when pressed against the side of the hand, should extend to the middle of the third phalange of the first finger, or Finger of Jupiter. Such a thumb would be regarded as of average length.

However, should the thumb be set high, it would have to extend proportionately farther up the hand to be of average length. Similarly, a low-set thumb of average length will not extend so far as the midway mark of the third phalange of the Finger of Jupiter.

The length or size of the thumb has a bearing on many personal characteristics. This applies strongly to the interpretation of hand types (pointed, conical, spatulate, square) or to the thumb and fingers individually if the hand is of the mixed type. Also the length of the phalanges shows interpretations when considering the thumb for size. Such data will now be listed in due order, subject to essential variants learned from the shape of the thumb, which will be discussed immediately afterward.

A long thumb is the indication of intellectual strength. It shows the person who can master situations and marshal his own aptitudes. It adds this strengthening force to other indications of the hand and palm. When very long, it indicates that the person will govern himself by mind at the expense of sentiment, often in a dogmatic fashion.

A short thumb shows lack of resolution, a weakness of both will and logic. It has a weakening effect on other indications of the hand or palm wherever will or logic is essential. When very short, it is the sign of the extremist, who resorts to an opposite course rather than face an issue.

A long thumb has a forceful effect upon the qualities represented by pointed or conical hands or fingers. It often pushes them beyond their natural bent. Therefore an average thumb is better suited to those types. A short thumb gives those qualities great leeway, but the person will need some strong association to show ability. Many a short-thumbed person in such a category has spurred on a long-thumbed associate to great accomplishment.

A long thumb gives an overabundance of zeal to the already energetic qualities of spatulate types. Here the average thumb is excellent. A long thumb is perfectly suited to the square type, giving all its practical attributes the benefit of forceful action. A short thumb with either spatulate or square types tends to wasted energy and idle talk about matters which are never accomplished.

The above factors are modified or specially interpreted by comparing the phalanges of the thumb. On a perfectly balanced thumb of average length, the first phalange is slightly shorter than the second. Should the thumb be high set and the palm quite wide, the third phalange would be termed as long. In brief, the hand, like the thumb, should be well balanced for the third phalange to run average.

The first phalange represents will power; the second phalange stands for reason; the third phalange denotes sentiment. Inasmuch as the third phalange forms a portion of the Venus area at the base of the palm, its qualities will be considered under that head in a later chapter.

However, when the thumb itself is short and the base, or third phalange, large, it is obvious that the qualities of the thumb proper will be subordinate to sentiment or emotion. This is why a short thumb is so often a handicap. Its mere lack of proportion, rather than lack of quality, prevents it from exercising its required forcefulness. Will power and logic may be inherent yet always swayed from action by emotional sentiment.

In studying the thumb, first define it as long, average, or short. Then compare the phalanges. If they are properly proportioned on any thumb, they show a balance of will and reasoning powers so far as that thumb's controlling force is concerned. But in many cases you can class one of the first two phalanges as long or short. Thus a long thumb might owe its length to the first phalange only; a short thumb might be such because of a deficient second phalange.

When a first phalange is long, it shows an overbearing

manner which can reach a tyrannical state. It indicates a desire to be active in everything, and this should be curbed. A short first phalange indicates a person who yields on issues, often by finding reasonable excuses.

A long second phalange shows a person who rationalizes everything, regardless of how he applies it. A short phalange shows heedless action, lack of tact, often with a refusal to weigh consequences.

Shape of the Thumb The average thumb is roundish, showing a noticeable joint between its phalanges, which often differ in their symmetry because of the type of the thumb—pointed, conical, spatulate, or square. The breadth of the thumb may be judged as normal if it appears in harmonious proportion to the hand. Should it show too much breadth, it is termed a broad thumb. The thumb is normally broader than it is thick; this can be noted by placing one thumb sideways in front of the other. In fact, the thumbs should be carefully compared all during this study in order to balance any differences between their indicated traits.

A broad thumb indicates a slow-moving determination, which may carry to great lengths but will resort to challenging moods should the thumb be short. Should a broad thumb be normally rounded, it will be both broad and thick, a combination which signifies violence in purpose, with a display of brute nature when roused.

Should a thumb of normal breadth show an equal thickness when compared, it is simply a thick thumb, which, though indicating a primitive urge, is usually the sign of a straightforward nature, unless bad traits are indicated elsewhere. The characteristics of broad or thick may apply separately to either the first or second phalange, being interpreted in terms of will power or reasoning qualities respectively.

A slender thumb is one that is less than average in both breadth and thickness. It can be best described as having a "fingery look." When long, it lacks its quota of forceful energy but makes up for it with a calculating patience. Quite often such a thumb will show an increased girth of its second phalange, which may be noted if the thumb is closely studied. This is a sign of wishful thinking which, surprisingly, may often materialize. It typifies the person who waits long for opportunity but does not let it slip when it arrives.

Often a slender thumb is of a pointed or conical type, which accounts for its first phalange being the more slender. When short, a slender thumb indicates a person with refined tastes but very little purpose; this thumb definitely needs strengthening from other interpretations in the hand. Sometimes a thumb of the square type has a slender second phalange; this shows a restless nature that can be controlled through physical occupation.

The waist-shaped second phalange differs distinctly from the slender and should not be mistaken for the latter. It tapers toward the center, producing an hourglass formation, though of course not so extreme. This is a token of brilliance and an ability to deal with people. Persons with this type of phalange are often very fond of animals.

The flat first phalange may be viewed when the thumb is held sideways. The tip of the thumb seems to "flatten" at an angle from the ball of the thumb to the end of the nail. Sometimes this angle begins almost from the bottom of the phalange. It represents a nervous energy that must be expended, otherwise the person will become extremely irritable. The larger the first phalange, the more physical activity such a person will require. This type is sometimes called the "nervous thumb."

A knotty joint between the thumb phalanges denotes (as with the fingers) analytical thought and accuracy in detail. With the thumb, this is highly important, as the thumb phalanges themselves represent affairs of the intellect. The influence of such a knot is so strong that it can retard the impulsive tendencies of smooth fingers. Therefore this should be carefully checked for later reference when the fingers are considered in relation to the mounts. A knot strengthens a short thumb.

A smooth joint, with its impulsive trend, does nothing to strengthen a short thumb but is somewhat helpful with knotty fingers, as it quickens their individual types of analysis.

Thumbs with various peculiarities of shape have been given titles of their own, but these are apt to prove confusing and therefore do not need to be described. The indications already listed are sufficient for the study of the thumb and its shape, as told by its component features. Where a thumb is both very broad and very thick, its primitive formation is self-evident. Where such a thumb is very short, it is termed a "clubbed thumb," indicating a lack of will power and logic. But, like any other peculiar thumb, it simply fits the usual shape definitions. To single it out because it is conspicuous is therefore superfluous.

Flexibility of the Thumb In flexibility the thumb gives indications similar to those of the hand. It can be tested during the first survey of the hand, when the hand is spread flat and palm downward to learn the thumb angle. This is done by pressing the thumb backward at the tip. If it does not yield, it is a stiff thumb, indicating a guarded but often reliable nature. Considerable yield means a pliable thumb, indicating persons who are socially minded and inclined to reasonable attitudes. Extremely pliable thumbs bend far backward and represent a tendency to extremes along with many interests.

However, the flexibility of the thumb has much more bearing on a person's character than that of the hand, and therefore should be tested separately to check for any variation. The thumb shows how far will power and logic will be applied to the abilities and talents indicated by the palm and fingers.

Where there is a long first phalange, a person is likely to

let his will power go to extremes if he has an extremely pliable thumb. This can harm his business, talents, even his health, unless such indications are heeded. Also, the presence of strengthening factors in the palm may be used to advantage. Often extreme tendencies may be diverted into less harmful or even useful channels.

The same rules will apply in other cases, according to the specific indications of the other phalanges, or any of the details learned through a study of the thumb. Flexibility, considered in connection with any features of the thumb, offers numerous examples as to their probable application.

Other Thumb Features With the thumb as with the hand, the classification of hard, firm, soft, or flabby apply with the same interpretations. Here again the thumb must be tested independently, pressing it from all sides to learn the degree of consistency. Often the thumb differs from the hand in consistency, frequently inclining more toward the firm or hard.

Thumbnails are classified and interpreted the same as fingernails. In brief, they show the following dispositions: short—critical; wide—outspoken; narrow—secretive; curved—jealous; fluted—nervous; ridged—irritable; tilted —talented.

These minor indications frequently add that bit of characterization which completes a person's individuality or gives a key to the application or shortcoming of some major trait. Detailed study is valuable with the thumb and becomes more intriguing the more it is pursued, for it is only after the observation of many thumbs that an analyst realizes the great amount of individualism that is expressed thereby.

In the thumb you will find the answer to many baffling problems of personality. Often a person of engaging manner will have hands which are appropriately expressive and show good character in the palm and fingers. Yet such a person may be unable to apply his natural aptitudes and will find himself continually misplaced. Generally the thumb indicates the weaknesses which retard such a personality. Conversely, a strong thumb will illuminate all the favorable qualities of the hand or palm and turn them into high lights.

Summing up the thumb, these facts should be remembered: The thumb is indicative of a person's fundamental character, because it shows how strongly will power and reasoning ability will motivate his capabilities. The very driving force of the thumb sustains a person's morale, and strong-thumbed people will neither accept nor recognize defeat.

With a strong thumb, a person can make his own opportunities. He may find himself stronger in determination than logic, or vice versa, and should arrange his campaigns accordingly. For example, a person of determination, as indicated by a long first phalange, should go after what he wants, rather than spend time reasoning out how he should go about it. With a thumb that emphasizes logic, through its long second phalange, a person who thinks out a plan beforehand will usually find that obstacles melt along his path to opportunity.

With a weak thumb, most notably a short thumb, a person is likely to become a defeatist. Such a person usually fails either to force an opportunity or create one. His best course is to develop his natural aptitudes and make perseverance his continual goal. Once recognized, he is judged by the amount he can offer, hence the more he has applied himself, the greater his chances of success.

At this stage in the study of a person's hands each thumb must be considered as subjective or objective, according to its corresponding palm. Here the rule of left and right begins to apply. With a right-handed person, the left is the subjective palm and the right the objective palm. With a left-handed person, this rule is reversed.

The subjective thumb shows the mental force that will be applied to the inherent abilities represented by the subjective palm, the qualities with which a person is naturally endowed. The objective thumb gives the same force to the tendencies shown in the objective palm, whose readings reveal how certain qualities are apt to be applied or neglected. In this case a person's age must be considered. In youth, the objective palm more often indicates what a person will do, whereas with age it carries a message of what has been done.

Summary of Chapter 5

As the link between hand and palm analysis, the thumb provides the key to the emotional qualities of the individual. Its third phalange is actually the palm area known as the Mount of Venus, indicative of a person's fundamental character. Therefore you can "set" an entire palm reading from the thumb.

High, medium, or low set, the thumb runs from a cautious to a careless nature. A long thumb shows intellectual strength, but when very long it reveals a lack of sentiment. A short thumb shows lack of resolution, and persons possessing this type will not face issues.

Though you will find long thumbs great strengtheners of character, they may prove too forceful with pointed or conical types, and sometimes with the spatulate. The long thumb is perfectly suited to the square type. In all instances you will find a short thumb a disadvantage.

Will power, reason, and sentiment are represented in that order by the first, second, and third phalanges of the thumb. These reveal interesting traits. Those of the third phalange are reserved for discussion under the Mount of Venus.

When broad, a thumb shows a slow determination; thick, a primitive urge; slender, patience. With waisted second phalange, you find brilliance; a flat first phalange reveals a nervous nature. Flexibility, consistency of thumb, and formation of thumbnails give minor indications.

CHAPTER 6

THE NINE AREAS OF THE PALM

In palm analysis, the keynotes to character are found in the elevations and depressions on the palm itself. Any noticeable rises or cushions are termed "mounts," and it is in accordance with their location that a person's character is gauged.

The palm is divided into nine distinct areas. Eight of these are defined as mounts because they are apt to be cushioned. They surround the ninth area, known as the Plain of Mars, which occupies the hollow of the hand.

Four of these "mount" areas are located just below the fingers and counting from the first or index finger are called Jupiter, Saturn, Apollo, and Mercury. They occupy the space from the base of the finger to the position of the joint or knuckle on the back of the hand.

The bottom portion of the palm is divided into two large areas. One is called the Mount of Luna. It occupies the outside base of the palm. Directly opposite is the base of the thumb, which in its entirety is termed the Mount of Venus.

Between the Mounts of Jupiter and Venus is an area called the Lower Mount of Mars. Between the Mounts of Mercury and Luna is the Upper Mount of Mars. The terms "Lower" and "Upper" are used because one is located below the Line of the Head while the other is above it.

50

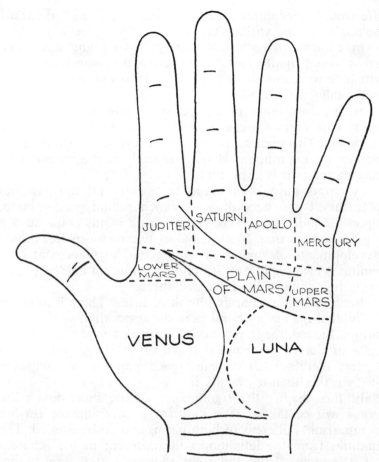

Each Mount of Mars has its individual interpretation. These two mounts flank the Plain of Mars, which as a separate area in itself has its own significance and will be discussed along with the other areas.

On a palm of positive balance there would be an equal rise in each of the eight "mount" areas. This would indicate a person of a harmonious, complacent disposition whose life would incorporate an exact distribution of all the traits belonging to the various areas.

In contrast, a palm completely lacking any cushioned areas would signify the utter negative, a person whose only attribute would be the lack of such. It would mean balance, but totally without weight.

Such palms, however, are seldom if ever seen. In almost every case certain areas show development at the expense of others. This marks a person according to the traits of the predominating mounts. Hence the study of the mounts is as fascinating as it is important.

Attempts have been made to classify all persons into planetary types, according to which mount predominates upon the individual palm. Only in rare hands could such a rigid rule hold true. In most palms two or more areas show developments of similar prominence. The placement of a mount is also important; it may carry into an adjacent area, imparting some of its influence there.

Each palm is a separate "Book of Life." There is as much individuality in every hand as in the impression of its fingerprints. Indeed, the imprint of an entire palm shows a multitude of differences beyond those of the fingerprints. It is better, therefore, to consider each palm as a composite study rather than to classify it.

In this chapter the significance of the individual palm areas will be taken, each in turn, as a guide for further comparison. All areas of both palms should be studied. The findings from the left hand will represent natural characteristics; those from the right their potential application. This is the case with right-handed persons; with those who are left-handed the order is reversed.

Considerable study of many palms is necessary to recognize well-developed mounts or their absence. The general rules of observation run as follows:

If an area shows a noticeable rise, it is considered as developed. If well placed in the area, this rise or mount follows the normal interpretation.

A flat or hollow area denotes absence of the mount. Should this be confined solely to the center of the area, it is considered as developed, but modified by adjoining mounts.

If the center of a mount is furrowed or divided by one or more lines, it is regarded as developed; but such lines have special influence which will be discussed in a later chapter.

It is important to note that the degree of a mount's development indicates, in turn, the strength of a person's traits. This brings us, however, to another phase: that of overdevelopment.

Just as any excess may prove injurious, so will you find palms that show an overbalance in some particular area. This invariably shows too much indulgence in a given trait. Here you will find warnings, weaknesses of nature.

A mount is overdeveloped when it is unusually high and spread over the entire area. If flabby or badly marked, it is also overdeveloped.

The mount areas should be studied according to the fingers that control them. The Mounts of Jupiter, Saturn, Apollo, and Mercury are related to the fingers directly above them. The Mount of Venus is controlled by the thumb, as is Lower Mars. The Mount of Luna is controlled both by the thumb and Finger of Mercury. The Mount of Upper Mars is controlled by the Finger of Mercury.

The palm areas are interpreted as follows:

1. **Mount of Jupiter** This mount symbolizes pride and ambition with a natural ability toward leadership. When developed, it marks a person who attaches importance to all his undertakings. It shows innate desire to gain honors and distinction. Honesty is a strong point.

Overdevelopment causes pride to turn to arrogance. It shows a self-centered person whose natural honesty may become mere policy, to be dismissed when expedient.

With pointed finger. A developed Mount of Jupiter shows

high idealism, a desire for fine things. It denotes a strong inclination toward spiritual attainment. Persons of this type are humanitarian in deed and devout in religion.

When the mount is overdeveloped, natural idealism is narrowed and the individual should guard against fanaticism or intolerance.

With conical finger. A developed mount shows pride in artistry and an appreciation of beauty. Love of harmony is inherent, both in surroundings and companionship. This is a sign of talent, which is not always realized by the possessor. Often such persons will overemphasize some minor faculty, unaware that he or she is designed for something greater.

Overdeveloped, there is too much pride in small attainments, often producing conceit. This applies to artistry, no matter how trivial. Natural idealism demands perfection even in the commonplace, and persons of this type can become overbearing in minor matters.

With spatulate finger. Here the idealism of Jupiter is creative. Always active, never idle, it finds new forms of expression, no matter what the channel. Highly adaptable, people of this type seek a wider scope in everything they do. Through energy they gain what they want and therefore their creative talent is often devoted to enterprise, wherein they demand and obtain the services of others.

Overdeveloped, people of this type are inclined to brag and exaggerate their accomplishments, belittling the advice of others.

With square finger. A developed mount shows love of order, though the individual may often leave it entirely to others. Here are found the most practical of idealists, who keep to fundamentals and judge perfection in terms of day by day. This is probably the most frequent of Jupiterian types. They are the masters of practical detail who keep the world in tow.

Overdeveloped, this type mount shows people who are sticklers for regulations. They can become martinets through their exacting ways. They must be careful not to lose a greater perspective by struggling for too much perfection of detail.

ABSENCE OF THE MOUNT OF JUPITER. Lacking leadership or self-importance, this indicates an indifference toward ideals. People with the mount undeveloped should avoid all feelings of frustration. They should adjust themselves to life as it is, because it is not in their nature to improve it. When they observe flaws in the virtues of their fellow men, they are apt to exaggerate them. Their common fault is to indulge in ridicule.

With pointed finger. Idealism is present but latent—often the mark of a cynic.

With conical finger. There is an indifference to people and surroundings, which, however, shows the aptitude to be satisfied almost anywhere.

With spatulate finger. Lack of purpose in creative matters.

With square finger. A petty tendency when provoked by a feeling of inadequacy.

2. Mount of Saturn This is the mount of personal philosophy. It serves as a check or balance on the indications of the other areas. It is less frequently developed than the other mounts and is seldom found in excess. In turn, however, its markings are apt to be all the more important. Hence the immediate indications now to be described will be subject to later elaboration.

When developed, Saturn shows the individual to be reserved, fond of solitude and study. Caution is evident, with a natural reticence toward an expression of opinion. This is because Saturnians weigh all matters carefully and are deliberate in every action. Since they consider the bad along with the good, they are subject to spasmodic gloom.

Overdeveloped, this can result in absolute melancholy. It is the sign of the hermit or complete recluse. Fear of the future and the world exaggerates the hoarding instinct.

With pointed finger. A developed Mount of Saturn shows a superstitious nature which can grow to a complete belief in the unreal. This may find an outlet in music or poetic expression but will not be tempered by application to the practical side of life.

Overdeveloped, the morbid tendency is apt to take full control, with an intense desire for solitude that should be avoided.

With conical finger. A superstitious trend confined more to belief in ill luck or bad omens. With this type, brilliance may often result through the urge for study. Being susceptible to surroundings, these persons should choose the brightest.

Overdeveloped, the trend is mournful and pessimistic.

With spatulate finger. Scientific urge is present here and combines well with the serious traits of Saturn. Persons of this type are more receptive to outside affairs than other Saturnians. They like activity but chiefly in safe or secure occupations.

Overdeveloped, this type shows a suspicious nature, particularly within the confines of their own pursuits.

With square finger. People of this type frequently thrive on solitude and generally do their best work when alone. They are serious-minded and suited to professions requiring retentive abilities.

Overdeveloped, they show a pronounced dislike toward any form of sociability.

ABSENCE OF THE MOUNT OF SATURN. Rather than being negative, the absence of this mount discloses certain attributes. It must be remembered, however, that lines and other signs occurring here will present additional aspects and therefore must be considered in due course.

People with this mount undeveloped care little or nothing for the occult and mysterious. They are free with their opinions and prefer to discuss cheerful subjects. They are sociable and seldom like to be alone except when working.

With pointed finger. These persons either scoff at superstition or ignore it completely.

With conical finger. There is a demand by the individual for realism, particularly in artistic matters.

With spatulate finger. These are the type who prefer work to sociability, though they are merely indifferent toward the latter.

With square finger. Little or no desire to consider serious subjects.

3. Mount of Apollo   This is the mount of applied artistry. People who have this mount developed give the world brightness, gaiety, and entertainment. When highly developed, this mount is usually marked with one or more lines which may point to fame. A well-developed Mount of Apollo produces persons of enchantment whether their position in life is high or low. Apollo frequently typifies versatility, whether in the confines of the home or the higher brackets of art, theater, or business. This mount, however, depends heavily upon corroboration from other parts of the hand, inasmuch as it covers so many potential aptitudes. The people of Apollo love all forms of artistry and will become its financial backers.

Overdeveloped, the qualities of Apollo may become fantastic. Natural intuition reaches tremendous proportions, enabling persons to gain credit for knowing much more than they do. When their ego expands beyond belief, it not only carries itself, but is forgivable even by its critics. These people show a fearlessness that enables them to accomplish colorful and spectacular achievements. The fault or danger in this is the reckless abandon and the improvident nature which must someday pay the piper.

With pointed finger. The trend is toward the aesthetic, with desire for high art, which often causes these people to be classed as dreamers. Overdeveloped, they will go to any extremes to realize such dreams, which are generally impractical.

58

With conical finger. A flair for the unusual, with a visionary trend, carried into private life and every action. Overdeveloped, these people exaggerate their own ability and thus often fail to fulfill their own ego. This may result in their losing what they have already attained.

With spatulate finger. Here we find acrobats in mind as well as body. Originality is their long suit. Filled with refreshing exuberance, their creative efforts are of a dominating type. Spatulates are the most versatile and adaptable of all the Apollo types and can readily succeed in more than one field. They have a natural stamina that goes with their ability.

Overdeveloped, they scatter their efforts and cite past success as a form of future promise. Lacking judgment, they become boring and repetitious, thus nullifying their talents.

With square finger. Here is a more careful type; its genius shows practicality as well as brilliance, particularly on the financial side. Achievements of these people come more from effort than bombast. Even when versatile, they have the good sense to concentrate upon one thing. Often what they start in they succeed in, whether it be business, profession, or artistry.

Overdeveloped, this shows lack of discrimination. People of this type will think of money first and therefore fail to develop talent. Their ego often finds its outlet in a gaudy display of wealth.

ABSENCE OF THE MOUNT OF APOLLO. Despite the amazing gifts of Apollo, absence of development in this area is by no means a handicap. If people of this type have no talent, they seldom care. Frequently, however, they have talents from other signs, but not of the spontaneous Apollo type. Hence they are inclined to believe that all talent is acquired or is the result of practice. They measure values by their own mode of life.

With pointed finger. These are dreamers without purpose. They prefer whimsey to art.

With conical finger. People of this type appreciate beauty in nature. They prefer a sunset to a painting.

With spatulate finger. This frequently symbolizes a dislike for artistic accomplishment. These people regard the aesthetic as ridiculous.

With square finger. Here is an indifference toward artistic accomplishment. These people are usually interested in everyday matters.

4. Mount of Mercury This mount indicates the shrewd, clever thinker who is quick to put his thoughts into action. People who have this area developed are often of a forceful type, with persuasive ability. If the area is well cushioned, jutting past the side of the hand, it denotes the ability of the orator. This jut also shows keen wit, particularly in quick response. People with a developed Mount of Mercury can sell ideas as well as goods. They are often pleasant and friendly; but even when not, they have an aptitude for making money. They may be found in any of the professions and in every sort of business; invariably their financial capability will be present. They are quick to learn anything they undertake and as a result are frequently inventive. Their determination knows no obstacles. They will travel to far places if opportunity beckons.

Overdeveloped, this mount denotes the schemer. It often shows an evasive nature. Such Mercurians are sometimes superstitious, but in an objective way; they believe in hunches and turns of luck. They will exploit almost anything that offers a quick return. Usually this overdevelopment is modified by other signs on the hand; therefore its dangerous elements are subject to control. Otherwise it is almost impossible to divert an overdeveloped Mercurian from a path once taken.

With pointed finger. Here natural ability gains flights of

fancy that can build to amazing results. These people can turn small ventures into huge enterprises. They demand quality or substance in whatever they exploit. They have keen intellect, but they operate on a policy of trial and error. Overdeveloped, they talk themselves out as well as in. They become too enthusiastic in promoting new ideas. They think in terms of maximum instead of minimum where cash return is concerned and often overshoot their marks.

With conical finger. The eloquent type, loquacious with purpose. Fine orators and persuasive speakers are included in this type. They prefer the spoken word to the written one.

Overdeveloped, they will use any expedient to accomplish the matter of the moment. They appeal to sentiment to gain a personal aim.

With spatulate finger. A rare type. Here originality is applied to business matters. These people are impulsive, concocting their best ideas on the spur of the moment.

Overdeveloped, these people are unpredictable and know it. They are overconfident, believing that no matter how wrongly they act they can always think their way out of it.

With square finger. Practical people, who base their plans on common sense, particularly where money is concerned. They never exaggerate a potential return, but see that all of it is gained. They hate waste. They are scrupulous in all dealings and are quick to detect those who are not. They admire instinct but prefer reason.

Overdeveloped, such people may become unscrupulous. They are strictly schemers. Whether they apply their ability to right or wrong depends entirely upon circumstances.

ABSENCE OF THE MOUNT OF MERCURY. Lack of business acumen is indicated by the absence of this mount. Also lacking are the forceful characteristics that carry projects through. These people dislike to keep accounts and are careless in financial affairs. They seldom follow new business trends and they lack sales ability.

With pointed finger. This indicates dreams of big business but no active effort toward achieving them. Lack of logical procedure in any enterprise.

With conical finger. Involves talking and idle conversation. Inclination toward holding useless, lengthy conferences.

With spatulate finger. Unorganized business energy. Poor judgment in all finance.

With square finger. Pinch-penny tactics. No vision regarding money-making possibilities.

5. Mount of Luna Luna is the mount of imagination. Located toward the lower, outer side of the hand, its development can be judged in terms of size as well as its raised cushion. With some persons the outer or percussion side of the hand is almost straight; with Lunarians there is often a decided outward curve, which in overdeveloped mounts may be a distinct bulge. Any palm with such a curve is a Lunarian type, for this enlarges the mount even though the cushion be slight. If the pad is unusually high, spreading over most of the area, any indication of a bulge marks an overdevelopment. With less padding, the bulge must be extremely prominent for overdevelopment.

With the inherent imagination of Luna come other related traits. These people are restless and often nervous. They love travel and strange places. With this is frequently found a yearning for the mysterious. When unable to travel or experience the unusual, many of them become incessant readers. They like to be with people who interest them, but often ignore others. Their companionship changes with their moods, which often causes them to be regarded as fickle. Generally they avoid solitude, but since they are never bored by their own company, they often travel alone. They concentrate heavily, to the exclusion of everyone around them. When disturbed in this, they draw off by themselves in order to work or formulate plans. They are apt to worry, and find this their greatest problem.

When overdeveloped, they become discontented with

their lot in life. They will go to great length to gain change in surroundings. Their urge for travel becomes uncontrollable, and those who have the mount with a heavy outward bulge prefer not only to travel by sea, but love to live by the water. They shrink from society because they feel they are different from other people, or not understood. Their worry often takes the form of imaginary ailments.

Since Luna is under the control of both the thumb and the little (Mercury) finger, a strong thumb will bring out the best in a developed Mount of Luna and will modify or temper an overdeveloped area. A weak thumb, since it lacks will power or logic, will leave a Lunarian very much the prey of his own imagination.

The types given below apply to both thumb and little finger with a blend of traits if the two types differ.

Pointed type. Here imagination may become sheer fantasy. These persons can be impractical in all matters. They often propound strange theories and adopt weird beliefs.

Overdeveloped, these traits become uncontrollable and dominate the individual's everyday life.

Conical type. Here imagination generally finds expression and is tempered by common sense and intuition. This is often applied to creative ability. Persons of this type also show a highly romantic trend. Their difficulty is concentrating on one subject, as they love all sorts of change. They also try to do too much, being spurred by nervous energy.

Overdeveloped, they become extravagant. Conceit is also a common failing.

Spatulate type. These people are almost always overactive, but given a field where they can apply their imagination, they produce phenomenal results. They need restraint or they will overtax their strength. Inventive, they seek new fields of endeavor as well as ideas. They sometimes become nomads, continually wandering through choice. They have a love of nature because to them it means freedom.

Overdeveloped, their invention becomes impractical and they can become thoroughly dissatisfied with the world.

They are the type of Lunarian who really wants the moon.

Square type. Here we find a factual imagination. People of this type seek truth and delve into history. Through their imagination they can often reconstruct an entire situation from a few facts. They have a strong appreciation of music and often a talent for it. Their ability to visualize gives them capacity as artists.

Overdeveloped, they incline to the grotesque. They lack proportions in their endeavors. They are too impulsive in their work.

ABSENCE OF THE MOUNT OF LUNA. If this mount were totally absent, it would be a sign of utter materialism. The hand is extremely rare, however, that does not have at least a slight development in this area. Imagination, as evidenced by Luna, is actually an expansion of the basic will force that impels a mind to action. When very slight, as evidenced by a straight-sided, cramped, or almost bony area, the indications are as follows:

Material instincts; cold, matter-of-fact view of people; belief in practical matters; lack of sympathy; impatience with anyone who expresses new ideas; stodgy satisfaction with surroundings; dislike of strangers; general lack of enthusiasm.

These traits, however, are seldom found in individuals of the underdeveloped Lunarian type. Their lack of imagination curtails such versatility. They are apt to show a few of these characteristics and abide by them.

Also, the markings on the Lunar area are more frequent than elsewhere, because of its greater size. These are influences that will be defined later, and often supply characteristics that are somewhat similar to those of a well-developed Mount of Luna.

Thumb and Mercury finger types. Pointed or conical show imitative ability. These people prefer routine physical work. They are capable of copying things they like. Active instead of restless, they carry through many things that others start but drop. Spatulate (rare) or square type shows acceptance of life as it comes along. These people are the most settled of all. They are generally thrifty and reliable. Their tastes usually conform to popular or group trends.

6. Mount of Venus The Mount of Venus represents affection, kindness, and sympathy. This applies in proportion to the development of the mount, but any largeness which might be termed "beyond normal" may be detrimental in this area.

The Mount of Venus is located at the base of the thumb, extends toward the center of the palm, its boundary being an imaginary curve or arc running from the fork of the thumb to the center of the heel of the hand and terminating at the wrist. Most hands show some elevation at the base of the thumb itself, and if this should be anything but bony, it indicates some development. Thus the Mount of Venus, like the Mount of Luna, is seldom totally absent.

Normal development shows itself by a definite fleshy rise somewhere in the area, or a gentle rise over all. Any restricted rise is subject to special interpretation according to its particular location in the area; such variances will be covered in a later chapter. The mount shows a better balance and is therefore more strongly developed if the cushion is outspread.

Overdevelopment is indicated where an over-all cushion also shows a heavy additional rise at one location. This applies, too, if the whole area is heavily cushioned.

In addition, an outward bulge of the thumb base or a sharp, extended angle near the wrist enlarges the Mount of Venus and therefore adds to its development. With cushioning comparatively slight, this means that the area is normally developed. Plus considerable cushioning throughout the area, it is classed as overdevelopment.

With its quality of human sympathy, the Mount of Venus naturally spreads an influence throughout the entire palm. It has a close association with the Life Line, which is the motivating factor of human existence. The vigor that the Life Line furnishes will naturally be colored by the emotional side of a person's make-up.

Therefore, the expansion of the Venus area toward the palm proper is considered in terms of the curve shown by the Life Line, which describes a conspicuous arc around the base of the thumb. This might be termed the Sphere of Venus, though the mount does not actually have so great a boundary. Usually the Life Line includes the Mount of Lower Mars, which therefore has an emotional quality though it is quite distinct from that of Venus. However, this sphere, when large, denotes an additional development of the Venus Mount. When very close to the thumb base, the Life Line cramps and thereby restricts the Venus qualities.

Since the thumb controls the Mount of Venus, all attributes or characteristics of that area may be measured by the strength or weakness of the thumb, which shows emotional control or lack of it.

Love of family, home, and fellow men is the keynote of the developed Mount of Venus. Such people are unselfish and appreciate anything that brings joy to others. Kindly, they are charitable. They are patient, tolerant, and cheerful. They make the most of life and thereby find happiness for themselves. Harmonious, they are fond of music.

Overdeveloped, they let their desires rule them. They spend money foolishly and are generally wasteful. Happy-go-lucky, they show overindulgence to others as well as themselves.

With pointed thumb. A developed area indicates soulful love. Hero worshipers are in this category.

Overdeveloped, this mount indicates unbalanced emotions.

With conical thumb. This denotes more practical sympathies. Philanthropists are in this group. Professional people of this type devote their lives to humanity.

Overdeveloped, the area signifies a fickle nature—people who are kindly but thoughtless.

With spatulate thumb. People of this type make a display of love and affection. They feel that lavish gifts to friends are symbols of their generosity. They are often susceptible to flattery.

Overdeveloped, this type shows a sarcastic nature. They turn frequently to new friends and loves. They often expect too much for a favor.

With square thumb. These people are steadfast. Their love frequently takes the form of devotion. They are particularly fond of children. They are quietly tolerant and extremely patient.

Overdeveloped, they often lose or shun these virtues. They purposely avoid family and home.

ABSENCE OF THE MOUNT OF VENUS. Seldom totally lacking, the Mount of Venus, when only slightly developed, shows a cold though often friendly disposition. These people are calm, because they are not subject to emotions. They have an appreciation, often amounting to affection, for objective things rather than people.

With pointed thumb. People of this type see so many imperfections in others that they keep themselves aloof from love and affection.

With conical thumb. These people become devoted to their work. They think that duty is stronger than affection.

With spatulate thumb. These persons are distinctly self-sufficient. They feel that love is a hindrance to their activities.

With square thumb. People of this type show complete unconcern toward love and affection.

7. Lower Mount of Mars This mount stands for aggressive qualities. Even a slight elevation is indicative of development, but shows that the aggressive nature will assert itself only under stress. A strong development requires an en-

largement of the whole area, with a definitely padded effect.
Overdevelopment takes the form of a noticeable swelling.

Development of Lower Mars signifies personal drive. It is the mark of the fighter, both physically and in enterprise. People of this type will not stop at halfway measures. Opposition stirs them to greater effort. They have courage and stamina, which are displayed either physically or through nervous energy.

Thriving on strife, they sometimes become troublemakers. Lacking fear, they frequently put themselves in dangerous situations, often unwisely. Unless their natures are tempered by the development of other and favorable mounts, they should always heed advice before making what might prove a drastic move.

Overdeveloped, they indulge in violence. They seek trouble until they find it. Their self-will completely dominates them. They are often noisy and purposely quarrelsome.

The thumb controls this mount. A strong thumb adds judgment to the Lower Martian development.

With pointed thumb is found an idealistic courage that will fight for moral issues.

With conical thumb are found fighters devoted to a cause, such as preservation of home or country.

With spatulate thumb there is the fighting courage of the pioneer. Aim will be gained regardless of hazard.

With square thumb the military spirit predominates. These people become militant when duty commands.

Overdeveloped, any of these types show destroying traits, directed against the very purposes for which they normally should strive. All issues will be gauged entirely in terms of self. Persons of these types need wise restraint.

WHEN LOWER MARS IS ABSENT. Too much caution and frequent uncertainty restrict persons of this type. They are not cowards, but simply prefer to avoid issues. Fortunately, this constant reluctance is often narrowed to limited fields, as indicated by the thumb types.

Pointed thumb shows inability to assert personal beliefs; conical thumb, a great aversion toward becoming conspicuous or appearing in the public eye; spatulate thumb, a distaste for any physical violence, even when necessary or justified; square thumb, a tendency to let oneself be pushed aside and be subdued by threat or argument.

8. Upper Mount of Mars This is the mount of endurance and resistance. Situated on the middle portion of the outside (or Percussion) of the hand, it is like a connecting section between the Mounts of Mercury and Luna. When cushioned, its development is easily distinguished by comparison with those two areas; contrarily, any deficiency may readily be noticed.

If the outside of the hand is curved outward, this adds to the development of Upper Mars, particularly if the curve is most conspicuous at that point. When the side of the hand shows a decided outward bulge, particularly with cushioning extending over the side, the mount is overdeveloped.

Development of Upper Mars symbolizes the person who will not recognize defeat. People of this type exhibit perseverance simply because they will not admit discouragement. They are stubborn, but usually in a purposeful way. They seldom seek combat, but, when forced to it, will resist opposition to the limit. These people admire sound judgment and often learn to exercise it. They can carry on despite fatigue. They are particularly pleased when their qualities of endurance and stability are appreciated.

Overdeveloped, they become very brusque. They consider themselves misunderstood. They will provoke an issue in order to force a fight. Once aroused, they are almost impossible to control.

The Mercury Finger controls this mount. With pointed finger these people recognize ideals but do not see the pitfalls. They often stir others to righteous wrath or indignation.

With conical finger they are silent, strong in purpose. They never alibi a mistake.

With spatulate finger they are always on the move. They will accept hardship in travel. They will try anything difficult to gain prestige. They know how to force others to aid them in their aims.

With square finger they will take the hardest jobs. Their patience is equal to their endurance.

Overdeveloped, all these types may show cruel traits: the pointed or conical toward those who dispute their ideals or purposes; the spatulate and square toward those whom they command or with whom they are associated.

WHEN UPPER MARS IS ABSENT. Persons of this type avoid issues completely. They develop an inferiority complex.

With pointed or conical finger they are subject to a persecution complex. They are very easily offended.

With spatulate finger, which is very rare, they can show complete fright at threat of physical danger.

With square finger they weaken under slight stress. They particularly dread pain or mental strain.

9. The Plain of Mars The center or hollow of the palm, otherwise the Plain of Mars, touches on all the areas termed mounts and therefore has a distinct effect upon them. This area is quite as important as the others but serves as a balance (or lack of it) rather than a dominating factor.

The Plain of Mars falls into two basic types: high and low. It is always depressed in relation to other portions of the palm, but the "high" type is level rather than hollow. If the hand is held flat and a pencil is laid along the second finger to the wrist, and pressed gently with the other hand, the depth of the Plain of Mars can be observed beneath it and a "low" type recognized by the considerable space between.

Highly developed mounts will naturally make the Plain of Mars look deep, but this test readily proves whether it should be considered high or low.

THE HIGH PLAIN OF MARS. Such a plain has a relationship to the Mounts of Mars which flank it. It indicates a quick temper and an impulsive nature. This applies particularly if the major lines crossing it are heavy and of a reddish tinge. If in addition dozens of little lines are in this area, such temper will be unpredictable and there will be an irritable disposition toward trifles.

Should the Plain of Mars be free of these signs, the person will be able to control these moods, though a high plain is significant of strong spirit.

If the Mounts of Mars are developed, any moods of temper indicated by the plain will find their culmination in the characteristics evidenced by the mounts.

THE LOW PLAIN OF MARS. This denotes a restrained temperament, even when both Mounts of Mars are strongly developed. If low, but without a very deep or conspicuous hollow, such restraint should prove even and well balanced.

When the Plain of Mars is conspicuously hollow, it shows an element of fear, which, in an extreme form, can drive a person to great despair. Centrally located, such a hollow shows fear of the world of life itself. If the hollow is toward one of the mounts, the person will be subject to extreme uncertainty in the traits which that mount represents.

This applies whether the mount be developed or not. Thus a hollow toward Jupiter indicates doubt as to the success of personal ambition; toward Saturn, a mistrust of one's own philosophy; toward Apollo, a doubt of personal skill or talent; toward Mercury, fear of failure in business; toward Luna, a fear of imaginary problems or ailments; toward Venus, a fear of losing love or family.

Many palms have a low but widespread Plain of Mars

that encroaches appreciably into one or more of the mount areas. This shows a feeling of insecurity in those directions which may reach doubt or fear under stress. This applies no matter how highly developed a mount may be, except for that encroachment.

There is an appreciable rise from the Plain of Mars to each adjoining area. The beginning of that rise marks the limit of the plain's area, whether the mount be developed or not.

Summary of Chapter 6

Proceeding from a study of the thumb, the areas of the palm itself are next to be considered. Here you find nine divisions, eight of which are styled "mounts" because of fleshy rises which sometimes appear in such areas.

The mounts at the bases of the fingers are named Jupiter, Saturn, Apollo, and Mercury, and are characterized by the qualities of ambition, wisdom, talent, and discernment. Luna, signifying imagination, lies at the lower outside of the palm. Venus, representing emotion, occupies the base of the thumb. The two remaining mounts, flanking the center of the palm, are Lower Mars (aggression) and Upper Mars (endurance) at the outside of the hand. The Plain of Mars, or hollow of the hand, represents temperament.

According to its pad, or cushion, a mount is regarded as developed. This means that its traits (as listed) will be present in the individual. When overdeveloped, you will find such traits in excess. When development is absent, you can rate such areas from the negative standpoint. Such listings and their modifications appeared in this chapter.

Here, also, you will find variations in individual natures, according to the type of finger governing each mount. The nearest finger is always the controlling factor and the palm areas are interpreted accordingly.

CHAPTER 7

SPECIAL FEATURES OF THE MOUNTS

From the data given in the previous chapter it is possible to make a rapid though general appraisal of inherent traits represented by the average palm. Keys to individual character may be gained from each of the areas defined. In all the stages, from complete absence of a mount through slight, great, or even too much development, facts may be learned and listed.

If all palms followed a uniform pattern, this could be reduced to a mathematical proposition. The differences in palms, however, seem to be as great as those of people, making it impossible to find two that are exactly alike. Hence before adding our findings or weighing one against another it is important to check all deviations and cover all the fine points.

In discussing deviations it should first be recognized that there is no such thing as a "normal" palm. You will find startling marks of individuality on every palm you study. Equally surprising is the way in which certain salient features will link different individuals, running them true to type. Soon, through your own experience in palm analysis, you will be setting up your own guideposts, recognizing how certain combinations, absences of features, fit together like the pieces of a finished picture.

In studying the mounts you will find variations as to placement, markings, and other features. Thus the term Mount of Jupiter simply defines a mount which is largely in the Jupiter area of the palm. There is no exactitude as to a mount's location, whereas the boundaries of an area are fixed. It is purely for convenience that the mounts are named after the areas in which they appear. Only occasionally are mounts found in the precise center of an area and often they carry over the border of another.

These inclinations or placements show corresponding variations in a person's temperament, making it all the more futile to class people as Jupiterians, Saturnians, and the like. Where a single mount predominates, almost to the stage where it dwarfs all others, we could define a person as being strictly of that type. But these cases are very rare, and at that the type would have to be shaded, according to the placement of the predominating mount. This matter of placement, along with markings and other features, forms a subject of the present chapter.

It should be noted that when a single mount does stand out very heavily, it is sometimes overdeveloped and will show the excesses detailed in the previous chapter. In such instances a lesser mount—or mounts—may be normally developed and therefore exhibit fine traits to counteract those of the overdeveloped area.

Comparatively few palms show a single predominating mount. Generally there are two—or more—that may be gauged as equals. One smaller in size may show additional features that rank it with the larger. There are frequent instances when study through the magnifying glass will prove one mount to be more developed than another, but they should still be regarded as equal. To grant one mount predominance because of a scant margin might seriously underestimate the other's value.

Palms with two strongly developed mounts are therefore composites. A listing of their combined traits will be given in the next chapter.

First, the variants of the individual mounts will be described along with strengthening and detracting factors:

1. Mount of Jupiter Centrally located, the Mount of Jupiter displays the qualities given in the preceding chapter: pride, ambition, and ability toward leadership. Should the mount be developed close to the base of the finger, it indicates a person who forces his ideas upon others, often making enemies thereby.

If the Mount of Jupiter is down toward Lower Mars, and particularly if it carries into that area, it signifies that the individual will fight for leadership, often regardless of his own merit. Once in authority, he may become domineering.

Often the Mount of Jupiter inclines toward Saturn, extending into that area. This has a sobering influence on Jupiter, holding its ambition in rein. It points to solid ambition, based upon tradition or scholarly attainment. Such a person may become conscious of his own lacks and thus lose the aggressive qualities required for the fulfillment of his ambition.

A long Finger of Jupiter strengthens the qualities represented by the mount. When abnormally long, it denotes excess. A short finger shows a person to be impulsive. When abnormally short, it detracts from the qualities of the mount in general.

The following markings directly strengthen or modify the mount. Vertical lines add to the development of the mount should its cushioning be slight. This applies to independent lines which occupy only the area of the mount, not to any of the general lines of the palm.

A single vertical line is a strong mark of success in ambition and the gaining of honors. Its strength increases with its depth and length. Sometimes a single line will show a double or triple formation under close scrutiny. This is a token of artistry which can prove helpful toward success.

Two definite vertical lines show that the person can carry on two careers, with a good chance of success in either or both. If one of these lines should be very slight, it will merely modify the single quality of the other.

Three or four vertical lines, even though slight, show a division or scattering of ambition, often a deterrent to success. Many vertical lines are a loquacious sign, sometimes causing persons to defeat their purposes by too much talk, which can even indicate a nagging disposition.

Horizontal or diagonal lines show inability to combat interference; if numerous, they point to confusion of purpose. Where vertical and horizontal lines both are numerous they often crisscross and become a grille, which exaggerates a mount and stresses its defects.

A grille on the Mount of Jupiter shows an inability to avoid obstacles and a tendency to blame lack of success on ill luck. However, the grille is often modified by squares, where vertical lines meet horizontal to form such a figure. A square (or rectangle when elongated) does not have to be perfectly formed. It should show three clearly defined sides, but the fourth may be partly open. A square shows presence of mind and an ability to correct errors. It also indicates preservation both of self and ambition. Two or more squares increase this aptitude.

Other signs and markings that have less direct bearing on the mount will be discussed in a later chapter.

2. Mount of Saturn   The Mount of Saturn is usually less cushioned than the others at the bases of the fingers, hence does not have to be overprominent to be considered developed. Also, the area frequently shows rises verging toward the Mount of Jupiter, the Mount of Apollo, or both. Being in the Saturn area, such count toward the development of the Mount of Saturn.

Centrally located, the mount shows reserve, love of solitude, and caution. This is frequently an overdeveloped area, and when the mount is developed toward the base of the finger, all its characteristics become intense.

Inclining toward Jupiter, the Mount of Saturn indicates

a pride in scholarly attainment, a tendency to take all matters too seriously. Inclining toward Apollo, the mind may run to grandeur and splendor, with less of the somber touch. It must be remembered, however, that developments in these directions are more often traceable as extensions from the Mounts of Jupiter and Apollo and therefore must be considered under those heads.

The Finger of Saturn has a most important bearing on the mount, more so perhaps than in any other instance. Normally it is the longest of all the fingers. This indicates a predominance in itself and shows a certain development of the Saturn traits, regardless of the mount's development.

Abnormally long, the finger denotes a brooding, melancholy nature. A well-cushioned mount may be regarded as overdeveloped in such a case. Abnormally short, the finger shows a tendency to ridicule all serious matters, often as a defense against a lack of their understanding that the person is unwilling to admit.

Often the Fate Line comes directly into the Saturn area. This indicates a well-regulated life—a tendency to stay within certain confines. If it reaches the Finger of Saturn, it indicates an inability to escape from such a pattern. When the Fate Line is accompanied by a well-defined vertical line in the Saturn area, it means brilliant accomplishment in that restricted field or life pattern.

A single vertical line has something of the same meaning on its own. It has often been regarded as a line of luck, but more logically it shows ability to find opportunity within one's own range of circumstance. Substantiating this is the fact that such good fortune is often gained late in life.

With two vertical lines, the achievement comes only through the result of long and arduous labor. Three or more vertical lines show an indecision counteracting chances of achievement. The more the lines, the more the person may complain about ill luck, which is another reason why a single line has been given a "lucky" interpretation.

Many short, fine lines on the Mount of Saturn indicate

an extremely delicate mental condition needing assistance. Horizontal or diagonal lines show feelings of frustration, which can amount to almost constant gloom if the lines are numerous. There is an exception here, however. Should several diagonal lines form a procession upward toward Jupiter, one above the other, they show that the person may gain a place in life commanding high distinction. Such lines, of course, should not be grilled.

A grille on the Mount of Saturn is a mark of resignation that often produces the very disappointments over which the person is prone to worry, a condition which can become progressively worse. However, this is one of the Saturn faults that is most easily overcome.

A square (or rectangle) on Saturn is a highly favorable sign. Though it may not offset the imaginary problems indicated by the grille, it shows intelligent ability to ward off actual trouble or danger and therefore will counteract some disastrous sign found elsewhere in the palm. The more squares on Saturn, the better.

The relation of other signs toward Saturn will be discussed in a later chapter.

3. Mount of Apollo Located centrally, the Mount of Apollo shows full traces of the artistry and exuberance which characterize this area. Toward its finger, the traits are even more dynamic but there is a tendency to be eccentric in their display. These are the people who really demand an audience.

Inclining toward Saturn, the characteristics of this mount gain stability and propriety. Saturn serves as a restraint on the Bohemian desires of the Apollo nature. Inclining toward Mercury, good business sense will prevail in artistic matters. This is the best placement for the Mount of Apollo. If the mount carries into the Saturn or Apollo areas (as is frequent with an inclination), the traits mentioned are highly evident.

Abnormally long, the Finger of Apollo shows over-confidence and a gambling instinct. Here is the attitude of "Easy come, easy go" based on a person's belief that he can easily recoup any losses. Though misunderstood by the world, these people, by their very daring, are often following their only road to success. Abnormally short, the finger indicates a lack of interest in one's own talents.

A long or deep single line on the Mount of Apollo is one of the best signs of the palm. Often this is a continuation of the Line of Apollo, which stands for success. If deep, this line will actually cleave a cushioned mount, but that adds to the mount's development instead of lessening it.

Wealth and fame can result from this line because it shows a person's ability to make the most of his aptitudes. Often, however, these will be the result of long effort. When the line proves to be double or triple when closely studied, it emphasizes the artistic qualities of Apollo, indicating that the person should surely follow them. Once called the Lines of Reputation, this multiple formation was regarded as an absolute sign of success through artistry or talent.

Small vertical lines completely separate from the strong single line mentioned represent a diffusion of talents, increasing with their number. They signify that the person should avoid letting anything interfere with his inspiration or most effective talent. Often the interference is his own; he will let himself be diverted by other interests or instincts.

Horizontal lines in this area show inability to surmount obstacles, which can prove serious with the Apollo temperament, turning toward talent as it does. Diagonal lines indicate lesser problems that can be easily surmounted.

A grille shows a great tendency toward overestimating one's own ability. This is the token of those who fancy they have talents which they lack. Also of those who believe their own publicity. With the strong single line, a grille can be counteracted, provided the line does not pass through the grille. The line at least will prove that the person has artistic ability, though passage through the grille will tend to dissipate it.

A square (or rectangle) on the Mount of Apollo shows good judgment in valuing one's own talents, thus preventing others from commercializing it to their benefit. The more such formations the better. They also have a counteracting effect on a grille if one appears. Unfortunately, squares are seldom seen on Apollo.

4. Mount of Mercury Centrally located, the Mount of Mercury shows the clever, quick-thinking habits that go with business. This is accompanied by ready wit when the mount is placed toward the outside of the hand. Toward the Finger of Mercury, the mount indicates that the person's abilities will be concentrated on business or management, including that of the home.

Inclination toward Apollo shows a brilliancy in whatever traits the individual is able to cultivate. Business ability will be applied to talent. These people have a practical buoyancy and are persuasive speakers, though inclined to fancy oratory.

Where Mercury extends into Apollo, make sure that Mercury actually predominates, otherwise the Apollo faculties will control, as previously described. Where Mercury does predominate, the two mounts sometimes appear as one. In such cases, business or domestic life will be applied to fine things: art objects, flowers, decorations, or jewelry. Fine surroundings are also demanded in all endeavors.

Inclination toward the Mount of Upper Mars shows a stubborn tendency toward business affairs and household management. Such capabilities are strong, but persons who have them want no interference in their affairs.

Abnormally long, the Finger of Mercury shows sharpness in dealings and unquestionably overdevelops the mount, bringing to the fore the traits described under that head. Longer than average, the finger shows good business judgment. Abnormally short, the finger detracts from the development of the mount. Business instincts may be strong but there will be lack of judgment and management.

Vertical lines have varied and interesting meanings on the Mount of Mercury.

A single line shows great chances of financial success, since it points to ability at one line of endeavor—always an effective procedure for persons with good business instincts.

The form of this endeavor depends upon other traits revealed by the hand. A deep single line, however, shows a scientific urge.

Several lines, if strongly marked and parallel, show a medical bent, indicating persons who make good doctors or nurses.* If poorly marked, these lines will be influenced by other mounts, swaying the person's disposition accordingly. Irregular vertical lines show a smattering of scientific desires. If these lines extend toward the bottom of the area, they show carelessness in money matters.

All such lines weaken the strongly marked parallels. Should the irregular lines be very short and numerous, they indicate the incessant talker. Glib salesmen and chatty housewives frequently have these Mercurian lines.

Horizontal and diagonal lines are indicative of financial losses from careless tactics. A grille is more serious, denoting failure in undertakings. A square (or rectangle) shows a natural ability or foresight against loss and often counteracts unfavorable lines.

5. Mount of Luna Because this area is large, a normal development must show considerable size; namely, of proportions which "balance well" with a rather full hand. A strong development requires a large outward curve or bulge, hence it can be recognized on sight. The mount must show a tremendous spreading size to be overdeveloped.

The highest point in the area marks its inclination. Centrally located, it signifies the general imaginative qualities of Luna. Toward the Plain of Mars, the imagination dominates almost all actions, and when it is not realized, persons of this type often become irritated. Toward the Upper

*This is termed the "Medical Stigmata."

Mount of Mars, it indicates imaginative action of a more practical sort.

Toward the lower portion of the mount, imagination becomes creative and restless. When the mount inclines toward the Percussion, it signifies travel and change; toward Venus, romantic imagination. If the mount is most prominent at its very base, bordering on the Rascette (wrist line), the imagination may become fanciful and distorted.

Any long vertical or diagonal lines, even if broken, give strength to the mount, indicating fertility of imagination. These are usually some of the general lines of the palm, which accounts for their importance. One or two deep lines, or several light ones, show this tendency. If the mount already verges on overdevelopment, the presence of such lines will certainly throw it that way.

Such lines, crossing at opposite diagonals, must not be confused with a grille, which is composed of short lines, very close together, like a screen pattern.

Horizontal lines found on the Percussion (outside of the hand) indicate nervous tension, in keeping with the restless traits of Luna. The more numerous, the more the tension. Such lines, when carrying into the mount itself, were once interpreted as signs of frequent voyages, but these may exist only in the imagination; hence this reading is obsolete.

A square shows protective ability against hazards, mental or physical. A grille shows a confused imagination, often disturbed by thoughts of ailments.

All tokens of the Mount of Luna are dependent upon other features of the hand or palm. Its outlets are found through the general lines of the palm, which will be discussed in a later chapter. Hence an overdeveloped Mount of Luna must be weighed by other indications before being given a final interpretation.

6. Mount of Venus The Mount of Venus covers a large area, which varies on different palms according to the curve of the Line of Life which marks the mount's greatest extension. To be strongly developed, Venus should show cushioning in its entire area. Otherwise, the highest point will be off center and must be located accordingly.

Centered, the mount shows the full qualities of Venus. Inclined toward the thumb, it shows a person ruled by emotions. Toward the Rascettes (wrist lines), it signifies intense physical love and affection. Toward Luna, it often symbolizes a coarse nature with a self-indulgent trend. Toward Lower Mars or the Plain of Mars, it denotes people with a selfish, antagonistic nature toward anyone who interferes with their desires. All these indications apply chiefly to private and domestic affairs.

Curved lines on Venus that follow the arc represented by the Line of Life will be discussed under general lines of the palm. Vertical lines are of doubtful significance and importance; usually they are portions or extensions of a grille. The same applies to small, short, horizontal lines. A grille increases the ardent desires indicated by this area; often the grille spreads over much space, in which case such desires may become uncontrollable. When the mount has practically no markings, it indicates a cold temperament, given more to admiration than love.

Horizontal lines or diagonal lines that reach the Line of Life, or cross it, are termed Interference Lines. These indicate hampering influences in a person's life, either through health or family problems and responsibilities.

A square on the Mount of Venus is a controlling influence against the excesses so frequently indicated by this area.

With a normal thumb, where will power and reason are well balanced, there is an excellent control over the qualities represented by the Mount of Venus. The longer the thumb, provided it is well balanced, the stronger this control will be. A short thumb indicates a lack of such control, marking an impetuous nature.

7. Lower Mount of Mars Being limited in size, this area, when developed, seldom shows appreciable displacement and therefore follows the general indications of Lower Mars: aggressive qualities and personal drive. The mount, however, is modified by the position of the Line of Life.

Should the Line of Life curve in close to the thumb, most of Lower Mars will be above it, and the aggressive qualities of the mount will be applied to the ambitious purposes indicated by Jupiter. Should the Line of Life swing high, Lower Mars will be under the sway of Venus; in that case, aggressive qualities will be asserted in personal and family affairs.

Curved lines following the arc of the Line of Life will be discussed with the general lines of the hand. A vertical line, if strong, indicates boldness. A square shows cool thinking in face of danger. These are rare markings; usually Lower Mars shows only little meshes of stray lines, indicating a nervous tendency, or a grille, which adds to the fighting tendency of the individual but indicates antagonistic actions.

8. Upper Mount of Mars This mount, when well developed, may show an off-center rise, which indicates the trend that its forceful, persuasive powers will take. Endurance and resistance are the basic traits represented by this mount; but those can mean persistence as well, along with fortitude.

Inclining toward the Plain of Mars, this persistence becomes a fighting force, both in actions and in issues. Often this is hard to control and can prove very serious when the mount is overdeveloped. Toward Mercury, a person will apply his persistence to his business or profession. When toward the outside of the hand there will be a heavy bulge at that point. Aside from indicating an overdevelopment, this shows a huge supply of reserve energy, which will often stir to powerful action. Toward Luna, the Martian power sways the imagination, giving the individual the ability to transmit his confidence and magnetic force to other people. When overdeveloped, this produces bombast.

It must be remembered that the fighting trait is present

in Upper Mars, but it is innate, rather than exhibiting the constant, heedless aggression of Lower Mars. Markings, however, activate the Upper Mount of Mars.

A single vertical line denotes great bravery. With more vertical lines, this is marred by petulance over inactivity. Horizontal lines, particularly toward the outside of the hand, show a tendency to make enemies. On the Percussion (outside of the hand) toward Luna there is an active desire for constant change. A grille shows violent temper over which a square is a controlling influence.

The Plain of Mars is not considered separately in studying predominating areas of the palm. It is allied, however, with the two Mounts of Mars, which must both be developed to denote a truly Martian type. The markings of the plain will be discussed with the general lines of the palm.

If both Mounts of Mars are well developed, a person will temper his aggressive qualities with endurance and perseverance. This is a happy combination, provided the proper balance is maintained. Otherwise, particularly when both mounts are overdeveloped, there will be a conflicting nature, one trait often ruining the other. These are people who will act first and think too late. Conversely, they may hesitate too long before showing the action of which they are capable.

If the Lower Mount of Mars is developed but the Upper Mount is deficient, a person will show bluff with aggressive action and will be easily thwarted when the turn is called. Should the Upper Mount be developed but the Lower Mount deficient, the person will consider action but seldom take it, letting others pass him by. These persons, however, are equal to emergencies and will often induce others to take action for them.

The Plain of Mars and its relation to the traits indicated by the Mounts of Mars has been discussed in a previous chapter.

Summary of Chapter 7

In every palm area you will find variations in the placement of the mounts. By studying these you gain added inklings or variations as to character interpretation. With Jupiter, for example, an inclination toward Lower Mars shows the person who will fight for leadership. Toward Saturn, a development of the Jupiter Mount indicates a sobering of ambition.

Similarly, all other mounts are modified by the location toward adjacent palm areas. The listing of such variants enhances the study of the mounts and clarifies their interpretations.

Along with the discussion of each mount the influence of the governing finger is detailed. In this chapter you will also find mention of the more common markings that are found upon the mounts.

Vertical lines, as a rule, are strengthening factors, though they may show divided effort if too frequent. Horizontal and diagonal lines usually denote frustrations. Grilles, of crisscrossed lines, stress the defects of a mount unless offset by squares, which are protective signs.

These are specified under the various palm areas, along with exceptions and modifications. Thus a study of this chapter will give you the salient features of each individual mount as guides to further interpretations of the palm.

CHAPTER 8

THE READINGS OF THE MOUNTS

In the two previous chapters we have covered the fundamental interpretations of each palm area and the variations, modifications, and other peculiarities of those areas. We have shown the general traits signified by each mount or its absence with relation to finger types. We have also listed specific qualities of stronger mounts, together with adverse tokens that may be traced thereon.

As keys to summarize these the following may be remembered:

1, Jupiter—ambition; 2, Saturn—wisdom; 3, Apollo—talent; 4, Mercury—discernment; 5, Luna—imagination; 6, Venus—emotion; 7, Lower Mars—aggression; 8, Upper Mars—endurance; 9, Plain of Mars—temperament.

The strongly developed mounts all show their influence upon a personality.

With the undeveloped areas it is equally possible to list a table of subordinate traits, all on the negative side, which often may detract from the developed qualities. But it must be remembered that these negatives, with very rare exception, do not represent forceful qualities, but stand for the lack of such.

Now, having pegged key qualities for better or worse, the proposition is to blend them. That, in substance, is the purpose of the present chapter. Our first guidepost is the fact that on most palms two mounts can usually be accepted as of equal prominence or development. Thus paired, such areas or mounts may be checked by the combinations in the present chapter, since they detail the blend or balance of the represented traits.

The second guidepost applies to palms that distinctly show a single predominating mount. Should that mount completely rule the palm, the reading would be in its terms only. But should a second mount show considerable prominence—as is usually the case—the single reading should be modified by the blended description that appears in this chapter.

As a third guidepost there are many palms which show three mounts of about equal development. These should be studied according to the combinations given in this chapter, which will make the reading all the more comprehensive.

In any case, you will find that through the combinations given here the facts regarding any palm will automatically begin to form a character analysis. A check back to the individual mounts involved will become a natural process; from that you will begin to tally the earlier keys covered by the general features of the hand, thumb, and fingers.

The readings of the mount combinations follow:

Jupiter and Saturn This combination is very rare. Where it does occur, the Jupiter area will usually be more heavily cushioned than that of Saturn. Length of finger and presence of vertical lines will be needed with the Mount of Saturn to equalize its development with that of Jupiter.

Saturn here serves as a pace-setter to Jupiter's ambition. With this combination you will find wisdom in leadership, with caution governing all decisions. This retards any precipitous actions indicated by other mounts. Therefore a well-developed Jupiter and Saturn combination is a perfect counterbalance should another mount be predominating and overdeveloped.

You will find that persons having the Jupiter and Saturn

combination do not like interference but will listen to admonition. Often this type must work alone to achieve the highest success and honors. Love of solitude often accompanies such purpose. Good, well-balanced fingers and a fine thumb will support these qualities. Any poor formations or features will disturb this delicate balance proportionally.

Particularly with a long Finger of Saturn, with an unusual long third phalange, you will find a person given to extreme melancholy. Defeatism can overshadow all ambitions. Only a very fine thumb can counteract these moods.

Jupiter and Apollo   Here you will find an ambitious nature influencing a talented individual. Should either mount incline toward Saturn, a sober, scholarly element will be present; this is accentuated if both mounts so incline. Since the Fingers of Jupiter and Apollo are normally the same length, any noticeable difference will favor the mount with the longer finger. Thus the ambition of Jupiter can become the impelling factor in developing Apollo's talents. Contrarily, talent can dominate ambition.

A strong vertical line cleaving Apollo gives that mount enough additional development to surpass a Jupiter Mount of equal height. In this case the advice would be: Expand your talents, cultivate the best that is in them, and from that find ambition. It should lead to great success and financial security.

When the Fingers of Jupiter and Apollo conform in type, ambition and talent will be in unison. Since a conical Finger of Jupiter shows talent in itself, it adds to Apollo's promise of artistic attainment. In this case, should the Finger of Apollo be square, it would add a practical business side to the artistic combination, another token of fame and wealth to come.

A spatulate Finger of Apollo, denoting artistic originality, will be hampered severely by a fluted nail, which indicates the wasting of talent through nervous energy. A square Finger of Jupiter would do much to hold this fault in check.

Long fingers add ability for detail to the Jupiter and Apollo combination. You will find problems with persons who have this combination. Overindulgence in material desires is indicated by a shorter Finger of Jupiter, particularly when its third phalange is thick, flabby, and too long in proportion. A grille on the Mount of Jupiter is a serious sign with this combination. Its laziness of ambition will lead to dissipation over any frustration of the Apollo talents.

A crooked Finger of Apollo, leaning toward Mercury, indicates a strongly mercenary trend in all the combined traits.

Jupiter and Mercury In this combination you will find a potential happiness in profession or business; indeed these are the people who can make the best, if not the most, of whatever they undertake. Where ambition combines with discernment, the latter often translates itself in terms of practical common sense.

This is the combination of the organizer, showing people of political or sales ability. A long Finger of Mercury accentuates this trait. Long second phalanges indicate a practical application of these potentials. A Finger of Mercury of the square type shows that such people are direct in method, as they need to be. Other finger types are apt to be diverted from their purposes.

When the Mount of Jupiter inclines toward Saturn, it gives these traits a progressive studious side. With long first phalanges, the fingers show a scientific capability. A long Finger of Mercury adds an intuition that often includes business sense. If the Mount of Mercury is marked with several vertical lines, it is termed the "Medical Stigmata," and is traditionally supposed to be the token of the physician.

Actually, the features described earlier in the paragraph are the real signs of a medical trend. In addition, the person must have a strong Mount of Venus to produce the sympathy and kindness so necessary in understanding the sufferings of fellow men. A strong thumb is necessary and a long second phalange is advantageous with such a thumb, because of its reasoning indications. A hand of the firm type is also a strengthening factor.

The vertical lines on Mercury are more the token of the conversationalist. They may help the bedside manner of a doctor or a nurse, but such lines are seen on many palms that show traits far removed from those with a medical trend.

An extremely long or crooked Finger of Mercury is an unfavorable sign. It may change the ambition of Jupiter into pretense or ostentation, often bringing disrepute.

Jupiter and Luna This combination of ambition and imagination often produces people who wish for things far beyond their reach. Given a good thumb, a Mercury Finger of more than average length, preferably of the square type, they will apply their imagination in the most useful ways, both to themselves and mankind.

Here you will find the palm of the writer, the composer, and often the inventor. With the inventor, a finger of the spatulate type is active and effective, but requires an unusually strong thumb. Knotty fingers are very beneficial, retarding their impetuous natures.

Pride of achievement through imaginative effort is a goal often sought by persons of this combination. The restless, dreamy influence of Luna, particularly when overdeveloped, is the hazard against which Jupiter must struggle. Here an overdevelopment of Jupiter can prove valuable as a stimulus.

If Jupiter should incline toward Lower Mars, or Luna incline toward Upper Mars, the signs are quite favorable. Both inclinations are all the better, particularly if the Martian mounts show developments. These are the marks of fighting commanders, robust patriots, men and women of great practical vision.

With a small short thumb and a deficient Mount of Venus, the Jupiter and Luna combination produces an imaginative self-importance in the individual. All markings on the Mount of Luna have a very important bearing, favorable or otherwise, in the study of this combination.

Jupiter and Venus   In good hands this is an ideal combination. Here you will find people capable of the highest form of love and sacrifice. They are ambitious for the sake of their family and friends. When they show ambition for themselves, it is constructive and generous.

Certain faults are evidenced by the thumb. Where the first phalange, though long, is flat and set so low that it forms a right angle to the hand, it indicates a person who will use friends and family to further his own personal ambitions at any cost. Nervous energy teamed with improvidence makes such persons not only generous to a fault, but at the expense of others.

If the thumb is extremely long and stiff, these people become dictatorial to those closest to them. If the thumb is short, they lack discretion, but are easily advised or guided by friends and family.

A square on the Mount of Jupiter is very helpful in controlling the faults found in this combination. A grille on the Mount of Venus increases all indiscretion.

Jupiter and Lower Mars   This combination shows people who seek leadership through aggression. They can surmount all opposition because they never lose sight of their ambitious goal. A strong thumb, particularly with a long second phalange, will provide the necessary balance. A knotted Finger of Jupiter, with long first phalange, and especially of the conical type, marks the real leader. A square finger gives practical application to this aggressive nature. A vertical line on the Mount of Jupiter adds force to all such influences.

However, that same vertical line can give equal force to

headstrong, violent trends, as indicated by a short thumb, which shows a person prone to fight without purpose. Similarly, a spatulate finger indicates a person who will look for fights. A thick third phalange of the Jupiter Finger will curtail active violence because of its sluggish trend.

Jupiter and Upper Mars This combines ambition with fortitude. It denotes the spirit of the explorer and the fair fighter, though it is found in many walks of life, including the salesman who always manages to put his foot in the door. It needs tempering with kindness as well as tolerance, and these are found only through a fair development of the Mount of Venus. Here a short thumb, though curbing aspiration, indicates a steady, co-operative nature. Any favorable signs on either mount may signify some great achievement.

Saturn and Apollo Here wisdom restrains and guides a natural exuberance, though with a long Finger of Saturn this excellent combination may be hindered by gloomy trends. If such a finger is of the square type and has a long third phalange, the gloomy aspect fades, for this person can handle all the economic problems of the talented Apollo side. If the Fingers of Saturn and Apollo both have a long second phalange, you will find a fine business mind that can apply the calculative needs of any financial venture. A long Apollo Finger with this combination indicates a born speculator.

Saturn and Mercury Saturn gives a serious side to the keen faculties of Mercury, but too often the sharp, discerning person will use his gift of wisdom to build false and exaggerated claims. Good fingers balance these traits, but the best help comes from another well-developed mount. Given that additional factor, the combination of Saturn and Mercury is found on palms of some of the finest people in the world, for wisdom and discernment are a rare and wonderful team when applied to well-chosen purposes.

Saturn and Luna Studious, imaginative, and restless, people who have this combination often turn their minds to the most somber phases of life, sometimes seeking strange and lonely places to gratify their moods. Should the Saturn Finger be pointed, such a person is most apt to delve into realms of mysticism and occult sciences.

A vertical line on the Mount of Saturn often produces a morbid nature, that of a person who imagines that someone is doing him harm. Any lines on the Mount of Luna show that the restless trend may become a mania, making such a person almost impossible to live with.

Some strong developments of other mounts are always a great help with the Saturn and Luna combination, which otherwise may seek its own strange way in a spirit of self sufficiency that could lead anywhere.

Saturn and Venus Kindly, patient natures are frequent with this combination. It shows people of truly philanthropic qualities who will devote their lives as well as their means to humane causes. The finer the fingers, the loftier these traits. However, people of this group often show a decided pessimism, which they should guard against.

Should either the Mount of Saturn or Venus show a grille, intensity of the worst kind may grip a person of this group and cause him to spread unhappiness among those about him.

An excellent composite is found when, in addition to good Mounts and Fingers of Saturn and Venus there is a vertical line on Apollo and some development of the Mount of Mercury, though the latter need be only slight. This betokens natural musicians and composers who often turn their talent to ecclesiastical music.

Saturn and Lower Mars This represents passive acceptance of life. Almost any purpose may seem useless to persons possessing this combination, hence they seldom use their aggressive qualities to accomplish anything. Their lives, therefore, are often wasted in futility. Given a very strong thumb and a fair development of the Jupiter Mount, such people will shake off their own mental shackles.

Saturn and Upper Mars These are the people who endure the problems of life with a morose or melancholic attitude. They exaggerate troubles in order to satisfy their love of gloom. Pomp and ceremony impress them and they are often ostentatious. Particularly when the Saturn Finger is of the pointed type, people of this group will fight physically for their convictions. When this combination of mounts is overdeveloped, it represents a cynic with a cruel trend. The combative nature may be counteracted by strong Mounts of Jupiter and Venus, plus good straight fingers.

Apollo and Mercury This shows brilliance blended with aptitude toward monetary matters. If the hands are fine and the Fingers of Apollo and Mercury are of the conical type, a variety of talents are indicated, along with artistry. Long first phalanges on these fingers are a token of great eloquence. A long Apollo Finger indicates a love of bright color and vivacious music. If the hands are weak and have short thumbs, it indicates a gaudy display of crude talents. A grille on the Mount of Mercury or a very long or crooked Mercury Finger are bad influences on such a hand. Any of these may indicate a scheming trend which is often cleverly concealed.

Apollo and Luna Here is brilliance stirred and often furthered by imagination. Great artists of all classes are found in this group. Given a long Finger of Mercury with this combination, they will turn their talented imagination into financial fields, often with tremendous success. Fingers of the square type add a practicality either to the artistry or imaginative qualities of this group; sometimes to both. Persons with this combination often show advertising ability and skill at exploitation. Poor fingers or adverse signs on the mounts, particularly overdevelopment, show sacrifice of art and even business for immediate or personal gain. Such persons can dream up many ways to harm the very things which they should further.

Apollo and Venus A combination fraught with wonderful prospects. Love, sympathy, and understanding are accompanied by great brilliance. Appreciation of the beautiful is also shown by this combination. Add a strong Apollo Finger and a strong line of Apollo; the combination will produce a variety of artistic persons, in accordance with their particular finger types. A long Apollo Finger shows persons with a desire to risk everything to please those whom they love. If the Mount of Venus should be marked with a grille, it indicates a selfish trend, particularly toward satisfying one's own personal whims. A low thumb points to recklessness and often a love of show which may lead to disaster.

Apollo and Lower Mars This indicates a selfish desire for importance. People with this combination feel they must be noticed. They are effusive, often successfully giving the impression of being much more important than they are. They hate advice but know how to gain favors. Given a long Finger of Mercury (controlling Lower Mars) such people will turn their egotistical but powerful abilities to practical use, often through convincing talk and argument. This combination represents self-satisfaction; it requires some favorable accompanying development—such as Jupiter or Venus—to counterbalance or modify its trend. Should the thumb have a short second phalange, it indicates a person who will go to any length to attain notice.

Apollo and Upper Mars With all the fine qualities of Apollo, appreciation of things well done, plus endurance and great resistance, this combination points to accomplishment in any field, from that of the military commander to the housewife. It represents the person who can rise to any

emergency and remain cool under pressure, plus an ability
to gain admiration through display of such deeds. This
combination can be greatly weakened by a short thumb,
poor fingers, or grilles on either of these mounts. Those
show tendencies toward bombast, sham, or makeshift measures instead of real achievement.

Mercury and Luna Here business combines with imagination, showing people who turn natural ingenuity to
commercial use. The women as well as the men are practical dreamers who can start and develop new enterprises,
small or large. In fact, women of this group usually have
a restless urge toward getting into something that offers
commercial gain. Even when these mounts are not pre-
dominant, they are frequently well developed on the palms
of women who become designers, buyers, nurses, or en-
gage in other professional fields.

The strength of the Mercury and Luna combination is so
forceful that it often makes up for a deficient Mount of
Jupiter or short Jupiter Finger by producing an ambitious
trend of its own. A long Finger of Mercury, since it controls
both mounts in the Mercury and Luna combination,
strengthens the commercial trend; if very long, it indicates
wild schemes and get-rich-quick desires. With short thumb,
a short Mercury Finger or other weakening fingers, the
Mercury and Luna combination is also indicative of heedless ventures which may bring serious consequences, therefore should be avoided.

Mercury and Venus Business sense with love of family
makes this an excellent combination. It shows people who
are generous, but usually careful not to overspend. Pru-
dence rules sentiment, producing good managers both in
business and in the home. A short Mercury Finger represents quick-thinking business people, impulsive, but with
a good measure of intuition. This combination often emphasizes the talkative traits of Mercury. Here a thumb with

short second phalange shows a willful person who may sacrifice anything through desire for gain.

Mercury and Lower Mars This is a strong, aggressive combination where money matters are concerned. People who have it usually devote their full energy to business. They have clear, cold financial vision; they will abandon or eliminate any proposition that does not pay. Once they choose a goal, they will undergo any ordeal to gain it. This combination shows obstinacy, which is most evident with a high, stiff thumb. Persons with such a thumb will let obstinacy rule foresight to the defeat of their own efforts.

Mercury and Upper Mars Here is found the ability to make money or accomplish other purposes through sheer endurance. Whether in soldier or salesman, it shows the person who can always find a new mode of attack and will never turn defeatist. Many people of physical vigor and dynamic personality are found in this group. A short thumb, particularly when thick or stiff, shows lack of judgment. It also indicates a person who will fight about small things and haggle over money matters. With a long hand or very long Mercury Finger, this combination shows a person who will go to any extreme for financial gain.

Luna and Venus This combination should be studied more from the indications of the individual mounts than through their blend, since both areas are large and their developments, therefore, are variable. With a thin hand, a person is apt to be idyllic and impressionable; with a thick hand, there is a desire for comfort and physical satisfaction. These people are likable, frequently combining the spirit of the romanticist with love of home and friends.

Always looking for new channels of expression, whether at work or in their homes, they are often happy with their visions rather than accomplishments. However, their restless natures can divert them into strange whims and moods, sometimes causing them to make a sudden change of occupation or even transplant their homes. A full development of these mounts automatically produces a spatulate hand with its indications of activity, energy, and independence. When either mount is marked with a grille, a strong thumb is needed to control wayward tendencies.

Luna and Lower Mars Here imagination becomes aggressive, needing strong control, particularly through some development of the Venus area, to produce a sympathy toward other people. Also, long second phalanges of thumb and fingers can rationalize this combination, and the stronger the thumb the better. These are people who will fight to gain impossible goals but are often able to put their energy to purpose through odd or unusual occupations that satisfy their imaginative urge.

Luna and Upper Mars This is the combination of the explorer, the adventurer, the person who seeks new horizons. With a strong thumb, such people often turn their dreams into accomplishments; with weak or unfavorable indications, they simply become reckless. It is a good combination with any other developed area, as it will add the best of such indications to its visionary and enduring nature.

Venus and Lower Mars This symbolizes strong, blind devotion to family, friends, and any cause demanding loyalty. People with this combination cannot tolerate restraint, hence may often be moved to anger, and will most certainly fight to preserve their ideals. This combination is frequently a strong one in the palm of a volunteer soldier.

Since people of this category usually have strong will power, a long second phalange of the thumb is needed to rationalize it. This is particularly true with a short thumb of the spatulate type, for this indicates the person who is always at loggerheads, even with those he loves or admires most. A short nail, with its critical indications, shows a pugnacious quality with persons of this temperament, making them very difficult to handle. They have too much energy to expend, and, lacking the logic to direct it, they can become quite cruel in nature. Other palm areas should be thoroughly checked to find channels toward which persons of this combination can be diverted.

Venus and Upper Mars　Here we find persons of patience, endurance, sympathy toward all mankind. Their one fault is too much tolerance toward those who gain their sympathies. Usually they have quickness of mind and with a thumb and Mercury Finger of the square type they are highly practical, equal to emergencies, and able to withstand tremendous physical strain. All persons of this combination are immune to discouragement and will defend not only themselves but those under their supervision. They are forceful in love and business.

When the palm shows a strong development of the Apollo area, people of this combination frequently have a great desire for show and splendor; to gain such, they may set goals beyond all limits yet attain them.

The combination of Venus and Upper Mars also has its unfortunate aspects. A stiff hand or thumb, short fingers, particularly that of Mercury, with thick third phalanges and short, brittle nails, are all bad indications. Unfavorable signs—such as crosses—in the Plain of Mars, or a thick thumb, deficient in logic or reasoning faculties, are also serious tokens. These can add up to an uncontrollable temper and a blind urge to gain any goal, no matter how unreasonable or unworthy.

Upper Mars and Lower Mars　This combination has already been discussed in connection with these mounts and the Plain of Mars, because of their interrelationship. As stated, the combination denotes the ability to temper aggressive qualities with endurance and perseverance; but an overdevelopment will show a conflict of those traits.

Here we are considering the Martian combination either as the predominating area of the palm or as the counterbalance to another highly developed area. Should the Martian mounts predominate, the person is a strictly Martian type. Usually these people have fingers of the square type, with smooth joints. They are quick in thought and action, the sort who become active fighters in time of war. When these fingers are long, with knotty joints, they represent the executive type, capable of analyzing situations and directing others.

Bad signs, such as a high Plain of Mars or grilles on the Martian mounts, give these people too much aggression and may prove very serious. The Mounts of Mars should be studied individually along with finger indications, particularly the phalanges, to analyze such persons thoroughly.

As a counterbalance, any of the other mounts are helpful when well developed. This is because the Martian combination is a balance in itself, adding a forceful yet enduring quality to other attributes. A careful study of the various signs or markings on the mounts is necessary to learn whether the Martian trend will prevail or be absorbed. A good thumb and fingers are needed in such cases, otherwise there will be a dissipation of the Martian qualities.

Having covered the blends and conflicts indicated by the mount combinations it is easy to observe how each presents its salient points, plus other outstanding factors. Most important, however, is the process of establishing a basis for analysis, then looking for features that may high-light the good characteristics or serve as warnings against the bad. Very frequently, and particularly after comparative study of many palms, much of a person's underlying nature can be read through the details given in this chapter, but the process does not stop there.

With palms that are primarily good, a check of minor details, fingers, nails, or a complete review of the thumb indications, may confirm or lessen the findings of the palm.

Conversely, with palms that show weakness in quality or serious defects, certain minor aspects may be added up to helpful proportions, particularly as guides toward the control of troublesome factors. A slight development of the Saturn Mount, for example, might indicate a dash of wisdom or inclination to study that could aid a person to subordinate unruly traits predominating in the palm.

So far we have discussed the background upon which the final findings are engraved. The palm areas represent purposes, traits, trends—whether for good or bad, and sometimes either—which are strengthened, weakened, fashioned, or flawed by thumb, fingers, and certain markings, some of which have already been described and noted.

How a person will follow or forget those purposes; develop or discard the traits for good or bad; rule a trend or yield to it—all these are the subjects of the coming chapters. We have learned the attributes that persons have; how they will use them are told by the lines of the palm. Similarly, where there are lacks, the lines themselves may show influences of their own that will often counteract underlying weaknesses or supply a motivation to amend deficiencies.

In studying the lines, special mention will be made regarding their relationship to certain mounts. These are highly important, as they often have an interpretation bearing on the mount itself. This has been mentioned earlier; it will be discussed in full when dealing with the lines. Such indications or findings can then be checked back against the readings of the mounts.

This is another reason why the interpretations of the mounts cannot be regarded as final in themselves and therefore should be kept open to amendment until the survey of the palm has been completed. The same will apply to the study of the lines, because of the additional markings which will be discussed later and tallied both with the lines and the mounts.

Summary of Chapter 8

In studying the palm you will usually find two mounts of almost equal prominence that dominate the hand. Obviously you must then gauge a person's traits by the blend or conflict of those mounts. Where a single mount predominates, there are often two well-developed secondaries that, through their combination, form a counterbalance to the predominating mount. Also, where three mounts dominate the palm, a comparison of their blends is essential.

This chapter discussed those blends or conflicts and for convenient reference their keys are given here:

Jupiter and Saturn, wisdom in leadership; Jupiter and Apollo, talented ambition; Jupiter and Mercury, practical ambition; Jupiter and Luna, creative urge; Jupiter and Venus, family pride; Jupiter and Lower Mars, aggressive leadership; Jupiter and Upper Mars, ambition with fortitude.

Saturn and Apollo, restrained exuberance; Saturn and Mercury, practical wisdom; Saturn and Luna, mysticism; Saturn and Venus, kindly patience; Saturn and Lower Mars, passive acceptance; Saturn and Upper Mars, moody endurance.

Apollo and Mercury, brilliance in business; Apollo and Luna, talented imagination; Apollo and Venus, appreciation of beauty; Apollo and Lower Mars, self-importance; Apollo and Upper Mars, strength in emergency; Mercury and Luna, commercial ingenuity; Mercury and Venus, prudent sentiment; Mercury and Lower Mars, business energy; Mercury and Upper Mars, commercial persistence.

Luna and Venus, restless romanticism; Luna and Lower Mars, uncontrollable imagination; Luna and Upper Mars, adventurous nature; Venus and Lower Mars, blind devotion; Venus and Upper Mars, tolerance; Upper Mars and Lower Mars, forceful endurance.

CHAPTER 9

THE GENERAL LINES OF THE PALM

The general lines that appear on the palm are chiefly those which may be found in long, continuous, and conspicuous form, following established courses through certain palm areas, with variations that will be duly noted. Of these, the three basic lines, representing Life, Head, and Heart, usually appear quite clearly, though they are subject to certain qualities or peculiarities of formation which will be discussed in this chapter and which are applicable to other lines as well.

Secondary lines, when they appear, may show the same features, sometimes being even longer and more sharply formed than some of the basic lines. However, they have been classed as secondaries because any of them may be absent, brief, or very slightly defined upon a person's palm. In some instances the presence of certain secondary lines may prove somewhat unfavorable.

Included among the general lines are lesser lines, such as the Girdle of Venus, which is a semicircle in a solid or broken-line formation found on the Mounts of Saturn and Apollo; the Rascettes, which appear upon the wrist; and groups of short minor lines which are easily identified by their locations. Having special significance, they belong with the general lines.

All of the above will be separately listed, described, and

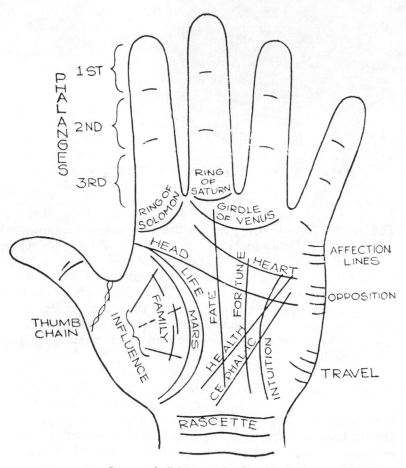

General Lines of the Hand

defined, in the chapters on basic, secondary, and lesser lines. Thus they can be studied individually in accordance with the usual rules applicable to general lines.

Any other lines appearing on the palm come under the heading of stray lines, and when clearly marked often bear an important significance upon the palm areas wherein they appear or upon the general lines which they cross. These strays also form certain signs, or combination markings, such as squares, crosses, grilles, and other formations, all with special meanings. Some of these have already been described and the rest—including some that are quite rare —will be detailed later.

Often some of the longer general lines show forks at their ends or branches, veering off from some other portion of the line. These are considered as adjuncts of the line itself. The branches, many of which are short, may combine with strays to form some of the signs mentioned above.

This brings us to the quality or appearance of the general lines, including their peculiarities of formation. The variations that will be discussed often evidence themselves in different lines on the same palm, hence they apply throughout the study of the lines.

A well-formed line is clearly etched through its entire length, showing regularity in its formation. By its very lack of peculiarity it strikes a note of perfection that is recognizable on sight. It stands out as though it were penciled by an artist. In color, it should be slightly pinkish.

Variances in color have been given interpretations. Red lines show more than usual activity but signify a tempestuous nature. Pale lines show lack of energy and a weakness of decision. Dark lines point to a vindictive disposition.

The length of each line should be gauged according to its own individual terms, which will be discussed in each separate case. Whether normal in length or not, each line should be checked by the palm areas on which it begins and terminates. The lines activate the qualities of the mounts, hence the relationship between the two is important.

Wide lines are easily noted, particularly when the spread increases at various portions. Wideness denotes a waste of energy that hampers active development. Deep lines, which become distinguishable after comparing many palms, show too much strain or tension on the part of the individual.

Lines very frequently lack the clear, unimpaired continuity that has been given as a standard. Many palms show striking contrasts in their own lines, often where the secondary lines are concerned.

When uneven, varying in width, depth, or color, so that at certain portions the line is scarcely discernible, it denotes an irregular display of the energy for which that line should stand. From the line's own measurements it is possible to determine at which stages of a person's career the bursts of activity have been or may be displayed, in contrast to the latent periods also recorded on the line.

A frayed line is one which shows very tiny lines fringing along it. Too slight to be termed branches, these fringes simply weaken the quality of the line. A chained line is formed of numerous and sometimes continuous links, all very small. More serious than fringes, a chained formation indicates a physical weakness in the period of a person's career during which the chain is active.

A double line is one that is divided into two distinct and separate lines, running very close together. This formation may be short or may run the entire length of the line. It is an excellent token, giving a strengthening influence to the line. In rare cases a triple line occurs, often fragmentary and with overlapping segments. The influences of such a line are variable.

A split is a dividing of a line, so that it forms two parallel sections which are joined at one end only, hence the term. The segment forming the split is not so clear as the line itself. It indicates a division of activity with a proportionate weakening of the line over the period it represents.

An island is a dividing of a line that joins at both ends. Though of elongated shape, it may be very tiny as well as large. It is a very bad sign which may indicate serious misfortune that can sometimes be avoided. An island, which is clearly a portion of the line itself, serves as a warning in the interpretation of a line.

It should be noted here that a study of the lines through

a magnifying glass is often helpful in determining minute details. A chained line, with its round, looped, or linked appearance, is quite distinguishable, and its components should not be mistaken for islands. Similarly splits can be identified also through the use of the magnifying glass.

When breaks appear in a line they show a cessation of activating force over a period measurable by the break. In some cases breaks overlap and are not so detrimental, showing only a change of conditions represented by the line in question. This shows a form of struggle in successive steps, particularly where the basic lines are so formed. Frequently a secondary or lesser line, which at first sight would seem absent, may be traced in faint but broken form, and its influence is variable.

Forks have been mentioned as the terminations of lines. Usually they are only two in number and are well defined. Unless the line itself is very weak, the fork is often favorable, allowing specific interpretations according to the palm areas that are activated by it. When the line terminates in multiple spreading lines, these are termed tassels, and show a scattering and diminishing of forces, which is always unfavorable.

Branches, already specified as small lines leading off from a general line, are favorable if they take an upward direction on the palm; unfavorable if they go downward. If a branch is clearly defined, extending half an inch or more, it warrants specific interpretations of its own. This is particularly true when it connects two general lines.

Signs on the General Lines In interpreting the palm areas certain strengthening and weakening signs were described, in the form of markings often found upon the mounts. Such markings, frequently composed of stray lines, also have a very important significance when found on the general lines of the palm. Some of the more common will be described herewith so that they can be noted when studying the general lines in detail. Others, which are comparatively rare, will be included in a later chapter summarizing the various signs and markings.

Forks, tassels, branches, splits, and islands have been discussed in relation to the general lines. Technically, these are formations or peculiarities of the lines themselves. However, signs and other markings now to be enumerated will also have similar interpretations where the lines are concerned.

The dot is a noticeable spot which may vary in size from that of a pencil dot to a pinhead or occasionally larger. It may be red, blue, black, or yellow. Dots represent physical defects or some form of ailment which may have a detrimental effect upon the individual. If a square surrounds such a dot, it will prove a protecting influence against the hazard represented.

A square is also a good sign when found at a break in a line, as it offsets any lapse in activity. Squares on weak lines are always helpful signs. A square can be irregular in shape, even rectangular, and one of its sides may be only partially formed, but all its sides must be independent of the general line on which it appears. A branch may assist in the formation of a square, but not the line proper.

The triangle, as a contrast, is a sign which may be formed by general lines in combination with branches or strays. Therefore it may be found rather frequently on certain palms and is of particular interest in connection with the general lines. Triangles are always favorable and are indicative of keen mental ability. They have various interpretations, according to their location.

Triangles are usually stronger when formed independently; that is, practically an individual marking, rather than as the result of the chance crossing of various lines. However, there are special triangles that have their own interpretation, being formed by specific general lines. These will be listed in a later chapter.

A bar is a short, heavy line that crosses one of the general lines. It is always a danger signal, indicating some serious occurrence or circumstance. Any stray line crossing a general line shows interference with the latter's activity. The longer the crossline, the more serious the interference.

A cross is composed of two small crosslines, both of the stray variety. Whenever any part of the cross touches a general line it is regarded as a bad influence, ranging from sudden misfortune to a temporary lapse of activity. A star consists of three or more crosslines. It has variable interpretations if it touches a general line.

A circle is a peculiar line formation which takes a circular shape, though it is very rarely found in perfect form. It has special interpretations when found with certain lines.

Comments on the General Lines   In studying the general lines, a comparison of both palms, the subjective and the objective, is important. The most effective system is to take the basic lines on the subjective palm, read them, and then do the same with the basic lines on the objective palm. The same process can be followed with the secondary lines and later with the lesser lines.

This is not so lengthy a process as might be supposed, because, as stated earlier, many palms show comparatively few of the secondary and lesser lines. However, it must be remembered that the lines in the two latter groups furnish corroborative or modifying evidence to the findings of the basic lines. That is why it is best to study the more important lines first. Throughout the study of the lines attention should be given to the qualities and peculiarities as detailed in this chapter as well as the special signs or markings.

Where corresponding lines differ on one person's palms, it is not difficult to blend or balance their interpretations. For example: If the Life Line of the subjective palm should show frays at the beginning, it would indicate that a person had been constitutionally weak at birth or during childhood; while a well-formed start of the Life Line on the objective palm would show that the person had responded well to care given at that period. Should the lines be the other way around, it would indicate a strong constitution during infancy that had weathered ailments or improper care.

Should the Fate Line branch from the Life Line on the subjective palm—as it frequently does—it would represent a person with natural tendencies to follow family tradition and respond well to early training. With the same lines separate on the objective palm, the person would follow his own inclinations or seek advice outside the family, once occasion should allow it.

Many such examples could be cited, but they will become fairly obvious when the varying interpretations of the lines are detailed under their proper heads. At the same time, it must be remembered that a marked difference between subjective and objective is not always translatable in actual occurrence. Sometimes a person will be governed heavily by subjective activities, never having found occasion to follow the objective indications.

Do not worry about mistakes in early readings. If facts do not coincide with your findings, look for indications in the palms that will explain the facts. From this process you will learn to evaluate various lines as well as other features, giving precedence to the more important. Do not at first attach too much importance to details on which you are not certain. The more palms you study, particularly the lines, the more you will be impressed by the amazing individuality each possesses.

With experience each new palm becomes a miniature panorama which you will mentally compare with others you have viewed. You will recall certain lines or other markings, as well as developed palm areas, which will resemble familiar scenes, and from them you will make immediate evaluations which may show surprising accuracy.

The old notion that the palm remains an unchanged

record has faded in the light of scientific analysis. Over the years the lines in the palm do change, as do some of the other features in a lesser degree. Splits may alter into islands. Lines can vanish, sometimes rapidly, and return. New lines have been known to appear. Certain signs have arrived after an unusual experience, as if marking the occurrence. There are reputed cases where markings have grown on the palm as the result of wishful thinking or the rise of a great ambition.

Much could be written on this subject, but its chief import is to show that palm analysis deals in indications, not revelations, and that whatever is shown on the palm is open to change, just as are personalities themselves. But a personality often goes deep, and so do the reflected messages that the palm portrays. One may be as difficult to change as the other.

Inasmuch as the lines activate and therefore are a governing force upon the palm areas and all the traits they indicate, we are coming now to the vital stages of analysis. While it is important in the early readings to check apparent findings with facts, as a guide to future accuracy or evaluation, the beginner learns very soon that the palm tells more than some people are willing to admit. Not only are many persons oblivious to their own faults; some are equally prone to grant themselves virtues that they do not possess.

It is good policy as well as practice to give a sympathetic reading, as it pleases people and subordinates their faults by emphasizing their better qualities. But the analyst who follows this rule will soon be reading and checking unspoken points that will test and prove themselves in progress. Persons who show themselves subject to the flattery that a good reading may induce will unconsciously be revealing some of the shallow or undiscriminating traits that the analyst will be finding on the palm at that very moment.

So do not be too willing to forego any findings that

112

someone denies after you have read his palm. Check your findings by reference to the book or by a tally with other indications of the palm itself, but check the facts that people themselves offer to dispute your analysis. You are likely to be amazed by the size of the percentage in your favor.

Summary of Chapter 9

The lines of the palm activate the various areas and therefore require a preliminary survey of their own. A well-formed line must be clear and regular through its entire length. Color characterizes a line: red shows a tempestuous nature; a pale line, lack of energy; a dark line, a vindictive disposition.

Similarly, width shows wasted energy; depth, strain; while frayed, chained, or other poor formations weaken the line's quality. Double lines show strengthened activity; a split in a line divides its energy. Islands and breaks are adverse signs. When a strong line forms a fork, it is often favorable, unless in a multiple form termed tassels. Branches leading from a line are favorable if they are upward; unfavorable if downward.

Signs found on the lines include dots, squares, triangles, bars, crosses, stars, and circles. Most of these are formed —at least in part—by tiny lines termed strays. Of such signs the square and triangle are always favorable. The other signs, with certain notable exceptions, are usually adverse.

In this chapter a comparison of a person's two palms is stressed. If you are right-handed, the left is your subjective palm, the right your objective. If you are left-handed, this order is reversed. The subjective is your key to inherited or natural traits, the objective to those developed or acquired.

CHAPTER 10

TIME ON YOUR HANDS

The time factor becomes an essential part of the interpretation of certain important lines of the palm. Each of these lines represents a constant activation of a person's natural forces, but there are periods when this is obstructed or dwindles.

All measurements of lines in terms of years are only approximate, hence any attempt to gauge them systematically may bring misleading results. For convenience, the lines are simply divided in ten periods of seven years each based on a line of average length. The spacings in all instances have a wider trend in the early stages.

Most important in terms of time measurement is the Life Line. As shown on the chart, it represents a seventy-year period. Quite often a Life Line continues farther and could theoretically be gauged as far as the age of ninety-eight. This does not mean that a person will live that long, any more than a short Life Line can be taken as a prediction of sudden death. It simply indicates that natural vigor, vitality, and as a rule the health that would be attendant will be present at those ages should they be attained or should nothing serious occur to impair them.

Early obstructions, often indicated within a span of a few years, which is about as close as they can possibly be

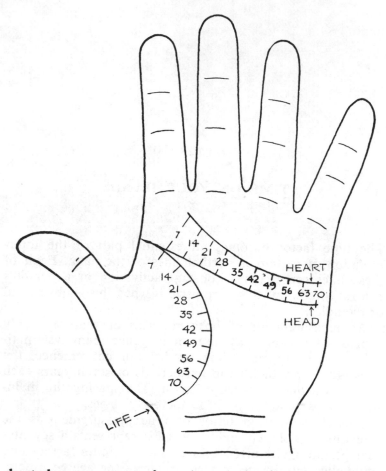

charted, may account for a later lack of vigor or health, contrary to good readings of the line. But usually the line itself will show the resultant traces and may even change with time. Similarly, a short Life Line, while it indicates a waning of vigor and health at an approximate period, may lengthen before those years are reached.

The Line of Mars, when present as a companion to the Life Line, is measured according to the same age periods.

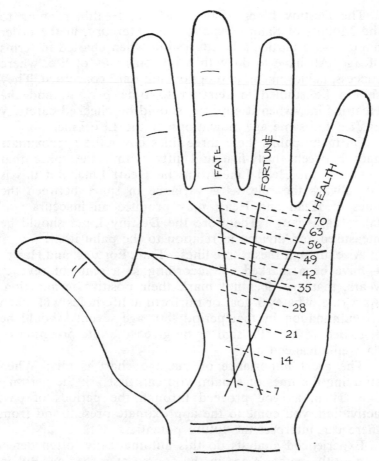

With the Head Line, representing intelligence and its application, the age divisions are charted largely for corroboration with the Life Line. The same applies to the Heart Line, with its emotional interpretations. Mental disorders and heart conditions have been ascribed traditionally to the Head and Heart Lines respectively; therefore their age periods may have a physical significance when checked against those of the Life Line.

The Destiny Lines—Fate, Fortune, Health, running to the Mounts of Saturn, Apollo, and Mercury, in the order named—are particularly interesting when charted in terms of age. All have to do with a person's way of life, where success, achievement, and opportunity are concerned. They should be studied in relation to time periods, and the Health Line, when it appears, should be checked carefully against the same age indications of the Life Line.

On many palms these three lines cover the approximate ages between thirty-five and fifty within the space that separates the Head Line from the Heart Line. But this is not always the rule, as a variance in space between the lines of Head and Heart may produce an inaccuracy if taken as a gauge. Therefore the Destiny Lines should be measured and divided in relation to the palm itself.

Also, though these three lines—Fate, Fortune, and Health —have been marked off according to a scale of seventy years, that age does not mark their positive termination. As a rule, whatever goal or misfortune life holds will reach its culmination by that period; but age seventy should be regarded with a plus sign or be given the interpretation of "a well-advanced age."

The great importance of the age chart is this: When studying the lines of a palm you can first ask the person's age. Then, as you proceed through the periods of past activation, you come to the approximate present and from there can interpret the future potential.

Experienced analysts do this automatically, often determining the person's age in the course of a reading. But in all instances past as well as future indications are inscribed upon a palm, though people often approach a palm reading with the enthusiastic question: "What does the future hold for me?" Actually, the whole analysis is a balance, a weighing of past and future interpretations.

CHAPTER 11

THE BASIC LINES: LIFE, HEAD, AND HEART

The three basic lines of the palm are the Line of Life, which follows a curve around the base of the thumb; the Line of the Head, which slants across the palm just above the center; the Line of the Heart, which curves downward from the base of the fingers and runs over to the Percussion or outside of the hand, below the Finger of Mercury.

These are called basic lines because they are not only found on almost every palm but they represent the three fundamentals of existence. Without life no one can exist; without a mind there can be no intelligence; without a heart the body cannot function. Thus these three lines are vital. But there are palms upon which two of them—namely, the Head Line and the Heart Line—combine to form one, which includes the qualities of both.

When this combination occurs, the Head Line dominates the Heart Line and findings should be gauged almost entirely in terms of the Head Line, with all qualities of the Heart Line subordinated. It is representative of people whose minds rule their emotions, and it may be cited as one of the strongest check marks of palm analysis. In this category you will find persons of an extremely practical or purposeful nature, whether their goals be right or wrong.

The three basic lines are divided into imaginary sections

117

which represent the years or periods in a person's life span. While rules have been given for gauging these periods, they are most easily checked by means of the chart which appears here. Three of the secondary lines, those of Fate, Fortune, and Health, are also charted. On other lines, time can be estimated, but this is not such an important factor.

Since the qualities and peculiarities of the lines have already been covered in detail, along with the more common signs and markings appearing with them, a detailed study can now be made of the basic lines, starting with

The Line of Life The normal Life Line begins at the side of the hand, between the thumb and the Finger of Jupiter. Normally it runs directly beneath the Mount of Jupiter, separating it from Lower Mars. Thus in the curve that carries it around the base of the thumb the Line of Life encircles both the Mount of Lower Mars and Venus. The Life Line should end below the base of the thumb, not quite reaching or touching the Rascette, the line which girds the wrist. If the Life Line carries to the side of the hand, it is unusually long.

Length of the Life Line is important, as this line represents physical vigor and its application to all life purposes. Therefore it determines the amount of nervous energy that may be expended in place of physical strength. Contrary to popular fable, the Life Line does not mark the span of a person's life. Such indications are more likely to appear elsewhere on the palm. Nor is the Life Line more important than the other basic lines of Head and Heart.

What the Life Line does show is a general vitality which, where weakened or interrupted, may indicate serious consequences through its very lack. Since ill health may be traceable to flaws in the Life Line, brought on by too much physical or nervous exertion, there is obviously some bearing on the person's life as well. Health, therefore, is a denominator of the Life Line. Where the line is weak, exhaustion is frequent and recuperation slow.

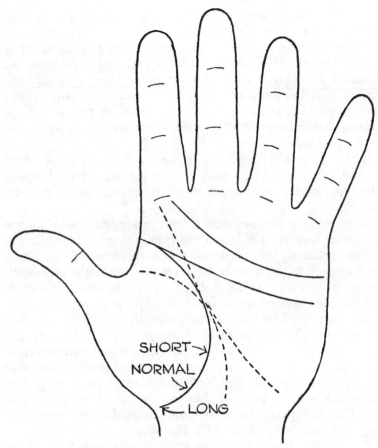

Life Line with Variations

There is a saying: "The longer the line, the longer the life," but this is also misleading. Where a Life Line runs beyond the normal length, it definitely registers periods beyond the standard age of seventy. This, however, simply indicates a natural vigor at a later age, should it be attained. Many people with short Life Lines live far beyond the age period at which the line fades; conversely, a long line is no guarantee of longevity.

There is also another interpretation to the term "The longer the line." When a Life Line circles well into the Plain of Mars, it is much longer than when it is so contracted that it practically rims the Mount of Venus. Since the age periods are measured by degrees on the arc of the Life Line, the larger circle shows a greater extent of line in each division.

The greater the curve, the more the natural vigor. With a good, clear line this marks the person whose vitality will stimulate others and it points to a strong, often rugged, constitution.

In contrast, the restricted line, cramped close to the Mount of Venus, will lessen the qualities of that mount, in a sense reducing its size. People with this type of line apply their energy to their own affairs and frequently lack sympathy toward others, not necessarily through selfish trends, but merely through an absence of expressive warmth.

Reading the Life Line from its beginning to the location of its normal ending or beyond one that is well formed and of normal length indicates a person whose natural vigor will show itself in infancy and childhood and sustain that standard throughout life. Very often the line is frayed or chained along the portion showing the first twelve years of life. This is representative of contagious diseases and common ailments experienced by the average child.

Should the frays or chains carry farther, they often indicate a resultant delicacy from the earlier period which will diminish in later years, though it may leave some constitutional weakness. Frays or chains throughout the line show a tendency to chronic afflictions and a highly nervous condition. Where the line has intervals of frays and chains, periods of delicate health or illness may be expected accordingly.

Where the line shows width, it indicates irritability or nerve strain, mostly under pressure. Deep stretches, particularly when red, are signs of a violent or feverish disposition. A thin, narrowing portion of the line is a warning of ill health which may be induced by domestic unhappiness, financial reverses, or other worrisome causes.

All of the above are vulnerable indications, subject to markings on the Life Line, or translatable in more specific terms by other data that are readable from the palm.

Fundamentally, the Line of Life indicates how a person will apply his natural vigor toward his mode of living. Much, therefore, can be learned by tracing the line and its branches from start to finish.

When the Life Line begins high on the Mount of Jupiter, it shows a desire to rule which often amounts to a tyrannical disposition. This is applicable to all types of affairs. Should one or more branches rise from the Mount of Jupiter and join the Life Line, great ambition is activated and will be applied in one or more fields which may be identified by the most strongly developed mounts or palm areas.

When the Life Line begins on Lower Mars or has a strong branch coming from that mount, an aggressive activity is added to the vigor of the line. Should the Life Line be joined with the Head Line at the start, it shows a conservative trend of action. The wider it becomes, the more reckless a person's actions may prove. Where the Life Line is joined to the Head Line for a distance representing its childhood period, so that it actually seems to come from the Head Line, it indicates a timidity and great sensitivity during those years.

Crossed or interlaced lines joining a separated Life Line and Head Line signify a childhood nature that shows extreme irritability when mismanaged by elders. Tassels at the beginning of the Life Line show a critical infancy.

Traveling down the Life Line, short branches should be noted. If these appear, any that ascend show the ability to continue ambitious or purposeful activity despite obstacles or failure. They might be termed symbols of replenished energy. Any short branches that descend show a diminishing of vigor.

Where the Life Line veers over to the Mount of Luna and ends there, it indicates that a person will travel far from his place of birth and will probably not return. This may be in spite of any desire, but if the Mount of Luna should be strongly developed, it will conform to a natural travel urge. A swing back of the line toward the Mount of Venus will indicate a strong desire to return, which usually will be fulfilled.

There is an uncommon form of Life Line which is often mistaken for a short Life Line but actually consists of two lines. One half begins as a normal Life Line, separated from the Head Line. The other portion starts from the Head Line itself and comes downward, either straight or curving below the Mount of Venus, and is often mistaken for a Fate Line. This is found in persons who in childhood were removed from one country to another, a small town to a large city, or vice versa.

Breaks in the Life Line, therefore, should follow the same interpretation: that of changes in life conditions but on a lesser scale. New surroundings, occupations, or personal motives may often be traced to the periods represented by such breaks, but always when they overlap. Sometimes a Life Line is formed by a succession of such separate segments. When a square includes the ends of the overlaps, it guards against any dangers or misfortunes, promising a satisfactory culmination from the change.

Breaks that do not overlap mean that vigor is only spasmodic, and show susceptibility to accident or illness, the latter often of a recurrent sort. Any square connecting such a break is a protective influence. This brings up the subject of other markings and their possible effects.

Among the markings an island is perhaps the most serious that can appear upon the Life Line. It is a warning of extreme delicacy or susceptibility to some special weakness. This can be identified if an island appears on another line at approximately the same time period. The Life Line indicates the effect; the other line the cause. The longer the island, the longer the duration of the trouble. Other unfavorable signs may appear on certain lines; they in turn will link with the island on the Life Line.

Where corroborative markings do not appear upon other lines, look for unfavorable signs on the mounts. Any of these which may be interpreted in terms of poor health are likely to show their influence upon islands on the Life Line.

Though dots seldom appear on the Life Line, their presence there is indicative of a sudden illness or serious occurrence. A branch line running from the dot may give the cause of this, either by reaching another line or pointing to a mount. Unfavorable signs farther along the Life Line may trace back to the trouble that the dot signified.

Splits indicate a weakening of the Life Line, but seldom of a serious nature. Crosslines show interference with a person's mode of living, particularly in early years, and may provoke complexes that will prove harmful to his general state of being. A bar is indicative of a catastrophe. Should the Life Line end in one, it is well to check the other lines in the hope that they show no corroborative sign at that period.

Crosses indicate an unhappiness, usually involving a close friend or relative. When low on the line, a cross may show a physical deficiency that appears quite early in life, reaching a later culmination. A circle is a similar token wherever it appears. A star warns against illness resulting from a sudden shock at the period of its location.

In defining the health hazards of the Life Line it must be remembered that they are by far more evident when the line itself shows vulnerable indications as described. A good, well-formed line indicates a natural vigor which often proves an immunity against ailments. A line that begins with frays and then becomes clear is very easily distinguished as one that has gained in strength. Free from chains, undue width, or narrowing, it can ride over many unfavorable signs or diminish their effect.

Dots or bars are always serious, but may be nullified by squares, if such appear in their proximity. Islands are always a weakening, but are greatly minimized if the line remains strong. The very vitality of a good line enables it to withstand shock and recuperate from affliction. Similarly a comparison of the Life Lines on the separate palms will often show a clarity of one that offers an antidote against the ill tokens of the other.

The Line of Life may be termed a motivating index, a dynamo that activates the traits shown by the mounts, fingers, thumb, and lesser keys to character. Where its power comes from, as well as some modes of its application, is a factor traceable through other lines. Associated as it is with the thumb and the Mount of Venus, the Line of Life is naturally a governing influence.

Triangles along the Life Line are symbols of alliance, sometimes representing marriages. Often they appear as portions of crosses; namely, when two points of the cross end on the line which thereby makes the third side of the triangle. This shows problems or unhappiness through such association.

Similarly, other indications may be gained from stray lines touching upon or branching from the Life Line; these will be mentioned later, when dealing with other general lines. But do not try to read importance into such markings unless they are fairly large and well defined. They represent the finer details of palm analysis that will become recognizable only after considerable study and comparison of many palms, with a check of findings against facts.

The Line of Head The Head Line should begin at the start of the Life Line, touching it or joined with it. It forms a gently descending slope through the Plain of Mars, toward the Percussion or outside of the hand, but should

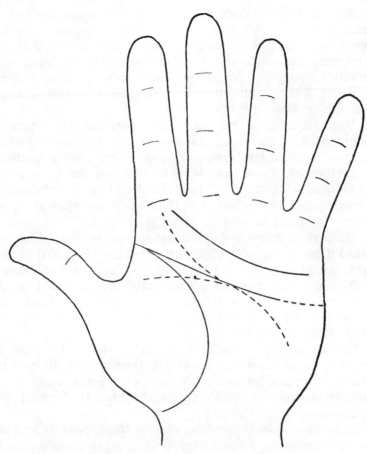

Head Line with Variations

not extend that far. Normally, it should carry at least to a point beneath the Mount of Apollo.

This line represents a person's degree of intelligence and its application. It is a guide to reasoning powers, intellectual capability, and concentration. These add up to mental activity, including memory, therefore this line is a great controller of a person's nature.

All mental functions are at their best when the line is clear and deep. When wide or shallow, it is less a ruling force. A frayed line shows that the mind may be diverted by unimportant matters; when chained, it often lacks continuity of purpose. Where the line becomes wavy or faint, it shows that the mind may be easily misled, often through inability at concentration.

Variants in color or width show uneven application of intelligence. The Head Line will show strength when slightly reddish, but when very red, ungovernable qualities are indicated. These have their effect upon the age periods as charted with the Head Line. Such indications should be considered in connection with the mental activities as represented by the line proper.

Natural caution and good sense are shown when the Head Line starts normally with the Life Line. Where the join continues, it shows timidity carried from childhood and may mean that the person has been retarded in his learning processes. Beginning above the Life Line, the Head Line shows a reckless disposition which increases in proportion to the separation.

Sometimes the Head Line begins in the very center of the Mount of Jupiter and veers or curls down toward its normal course. This shows conceit as the great factor in all mental processes and the longer the line, the greater the conceit.

Beginning from somewhere else on the Mount of Jupiter, or with branches coming from that area, the line indicates that a person is mentally ambitious, firm in opinion, and will resort to obstinacy to maintain a fixed idea. These active elements will be backed by other mental forces indicated by the line. Branches from Jupiter show strong application to the abilities represented by well-developed mounts.

When the Head Line begins on Lower Mars and cuts through the Life Line, it shows an irritable disposition which lacks dependability. Any branch from Lower Mars shows the same tendency in a lesser degree. Family ties or friendships may be broken when such markings appear. Should the Head Line start under the Mount of Saturn, thus having its early period missing, it shows a lack of early influence, indicating absence of pride either in family or achievements. In this category, which is very rare, are persons who care about very little and show a morbid mentality.

When the Head Line is straight, it shows fine mental control which will counteract or subordinate any handicaps shown by its point of origin. A straight line, when long, shows an application to detail if corroborated by other evidence on the hand. Curved downward toward the Mount of Luna, it shows an imaginative ability which is all the more emphasized should the curve increase and extend into that mount. People with such a line have minds which run to fantasy and can apply their mental prowess with remarkable results if the palm shows favorable traits or possibilities in connection with this. Otherwise, instead of creative imagination, this mental force will be wasted in foolish dreams. A Head Line starting high or with branches from Jupiter is helpful to the Luna extension, because the realm of the imagination can absorb the daring force or mental ambition which ordinarily would bring defeated purposes.

Head Lines that end in upward curves activate the mounts toward which they veer. Toward Saturn, this is a very poor token, because the line is short, showing an irrational mind with lack of concentration. Since such a line activates Saturn, with its scholarly qualities, the result can be a constantly morbid sense of extreme frustration.

Toward Apollo, the Head Line activates talent, and though it may be too short to supply intellectual vigor or concentration it can produce great personal brilliance, increasing with the length of the line. Toward Mercury, the Head Line shows a practical turn of mind; though often of the painstaking order, it still promises much material success.

Extending into Upper Mars, the Head Line produces a person of magnetic intellect, strong on perseverance and keen of memory. However, should the line extend clear to the Percussion, it marks an intellect so self-centered that all its force becomes secretive.

Forks or branches at the ending of the line can activate Mercury with its practicality, Upper Mars with its endurance, Luna with its imagination, sometimes in separate pairs or all three together, depending upon the particular line. This shows versatility with concentration and is valuable with good hands but may prove harmful where other indications are unfavorable.

Any pronounced branch extending into a mount directs mental energy into the qualities of that mount. There, however, lies the very substance of the Head Line's activating influence. Upon the development of those mounts or their absence depends the use to which the mental force will be put. When the areas are developed or show favorable qualities, they will be finely activated; overdeveloped, they will show extreme traits; absent, they reduce the activation to wishful thinking.

Comparison of the Head Lines on both palms is of great importance because here we find what amounts to two minds: the subjective, or inward; the objective, or outward. The first shows a person's own inner inclinations; the second, how he conducts himself in his dealings with the world. What seem startling contrasts in a person's dual nature are often recorded in the Head Line.

Breaks in the Head Line are sometimes very serious. They impede thinking and concentration, which may be owing to ailments. An overlapping of a break gives recuperative ability. A connecting square is a protective sign against serious consequences. Breaks occurring on a long line after it has passed normal length are more in the nature of added lines, showing additional qualities, like helpful interests detached from the general thought train.

Islands show periods of mental problems or confusion,

which may be dated by chart and compared with the Life Line to learn if the effect is serious. When they show on the subjective palm only, the absence of unfavorable markings on the objective palm shows the ability to subdue such inner strain or tumult. Crosslines are of slight consequence, but bars show tendencies to severe headaches. Dots show feverish spells; stars indicate mental shock.

Crosses may show anything from thwarted purposes to great mental grief. Circles are also of bad portent. Triangles are highly favorable, showing ingenuity and inventive ability. They apply equally when found on branches and then indicate the particular field toward which such capabilities may be directed.

Similarly, signs which are ordinarily bad upon the line proper will show favorable indications on branches, just as a continuation of the Head Line, though broken, is a good token. A star or a circle which appears near the terminus of a branch that actually leads into a mount will be a sign of great brilliance in the qualities of that area.

The Line of Heart   The Heart Line normally begins somewhere on the Mount of Jupiter, curves downward, and runs along the bases of the succeeding mounts, separating the areas of Mercury and Upper Mars, thus reaching the Percussion or outside of the hand.

This line activates the emotional qualities of the individual and also indicates physical conditions dependent on the heart. A clear, well-formed line portrays balanced sympathies and steadfast affections. With depth and color, it is also a token of a strong heart. Wide, the line shows passing affection, often stirred by selfish jealousy. Thin, it shows a trend toward admiration or devotion rather than intense love.

Frays are significant of a flirtatious disposition and often show a fluttery heart. A chained line shows an intensity equaled only by forgetfulness. Traditionally, it has been said to mean imperfect heart action which could account

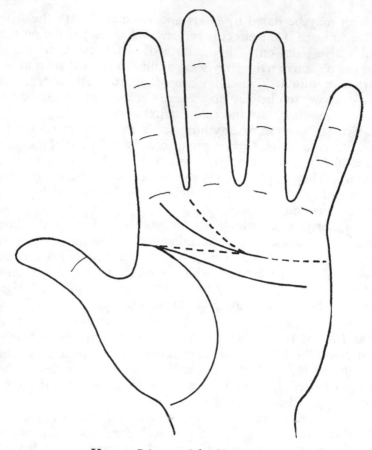

Heart Line with Variations

for unpredictable emotions. As with the Lines of Life and Head, the chart of the Heart Line will indicate the periods of its vagaries.

Starting from the Mount of Jupiter, the Heart Line indicates a person who will direct all sympathies and emotions toward ideal love, even at great sacrifice. When the line begins between the areas of Jupiter and Saturn, it represents a practical type of love, highly sympathetic but governing emotion with common sense, preferring plans to sacrifice.

Should the line begin on the Mount of Saturn, it shows that love is ruled by sensual emotion. It indicates a nature that is often forgiving and tolerant, with good judgment in affection if the line starts high on the mount. This is because it divides the mount and therefore partakes of its wisdom. In rare cases the line starts between the Fingers of Saturn and Apollo, or has a branch from that location. This in-dicates that the person's love and sympathy will be attracted by briliance. Starting low on Saturn, the line lacks all sobriety of that area.

The line may begin with a double or triple fork com-bining any two or all three of the usual starting points. Sometimes this is more a single line drawing in a thinner branch or branches. The strongest line predominates, but gains qualities from any others, according to their com-parative strength as gauged by appearance.

When the Heart Line begins with the Head Line, it shows an envious disposition, wherein the head rules the heart, often to the latter's discomfort. When Heart, Head, and Life Lines are all joined at the start, you find the person who will go to any extent to gain what he wants in love. This often results in great disappointment or disaster be-cause of unreasonable passion.

A wavy Heart Line shows unpredictable periods because when its dips come close to the Head Line it is ruled thereby. Branches from the Heart Line down to the Head Line show disappointments in love or friendship. These should not be confused with any of the secondary lines of the palm. If the Heart Line stops short of the Percussion, it warns against undue exertion beyond the period so charted. This should be checked with the Life Line. Ending in a tassel, the Heart Line shows a diminishing of energy, both sentimental and physical.

When the Heart Line rises or remains high, thus termi-nating in the Mercury area, it shows that love and sentiment are valued largely in terms of money. All sympathy may be applied toward activating the desire for worldly gain.

Breaks are signs of inconstancy; observed on both palms, they may indicate physical ailments. Overlapping, they show possibilities of reunion when love or friendship has been broken. Where illness occurs at those periods, overlapping breaks are signs of recovery. Squares lessen and sometimes divert these breaks.

Islands, like breaks, show variable or inconstant periods. Circles, dots, crosses, and other such unfavorable signs bespeak rifts, quarrels, or serious interferences in love and friendship, their extent depending much on circumstance. Here the health factor of the Heart Line has often been emphasized, particularly when the line is of poor appearance or formation. In such cases all markings should be checked against the same period on the Life Line to see if effects are registered there to tally with Heart Line causes.

Summary of Basic Lines

Double lines may occur with any of the basic lines. Sometimes they are very close together, in which case they give great strength to the line, one making up for the defects of the other. They are considered most fortunate whenever they occur. Triple lines also appear, but usually in segments. They show an artistic ability and offset the deficiencies of broken lines.

When there is considerable space between double lines, the additional line is termed a sister line. Such a line follows along beside the usual line and strengthens it. Secondary lines, which often appear in fragmentary form, should not be mistaken for sister lines. Such lines will be described in the next chapter, which covers the secondary lines.

CHAPTER 12

THE SECONDARY LINES

Among the secondary lines there are three of great significance which as a group can be classed as Lines of Destiny.
These are the Lines of Fate, Fortune, and Health; also
called the Lines of Saturn, Apollo, and Mercury, because
in their long courses up from the wrist and across the palm
they usually terminate at those respective areas.

Any of these lines may be absent from the palm. Often
only one of them is clearly defined. There have been attempts to interpret them as one line, its significance varying
according to the terminal mount. But if this were done,
either of the other two lines, when strongly present, would
show interpretations of its own rather than merely rating as
a sister line.

Hence the Lines of Fate, Fortune, and Health should be
separately analyzed. Often when only one appears traces
may be found of the others. Sometimes such traces are so
slight that at first sight they appear to be stray lines, but if
they follow the pathways to Saturn, Apollo, or Mercury,
they must be regarded as evidence of the particular line
that should take that course.

These three lines are charted according to age periods
which conform fairly closely. Hence, when one is weak,
another, if strong at that period, will support the weaker

133

line. Similarly, any of these three will supplement a short Life Line. Where a Life Line ends there can often be a cessation of the will to live, and when any Destiny Line goes beyond that period it will provide an equivalent urge.

A person will not "live on the other line" with the usual activating forces of the Life Line proceeding along this new channel. It simply means that the interests, opportunities, and culmination of efforts promised by the strongest of the Destiny Lines will prove sustaining influences.

So far our palm analysis has given general indications as applied to the qualities of the mounts or palm areas, which have defined or blended themselves in terms of ambition, wisdom, talent, discernment, and other traits. The Life Line has shown the natural vigor that may be applied to these, with weaknesses or obstacles, sometimes in the form of health. The Head Line has shown how strongly the mind may activate such qualities. The Heart Line has given the emotional application.

Now, in contrast to those ruling lines we are coming to three that shape our destinies, but only in so far as we are willing to let them. From Fate, Fortune, and Health are found the courses, outside forces, and stumbling blocks, as well as helps, which can account for happiness or unhappiness, success or failure, or the general fits or misfits that feature every career.

The Line of Fate (Line of Saturn) The Fate Line should start from the base of the palm and follow a straight course up through the Plain of Mars and into the area of Saturn. It is subject to many variations, however, which will be described as we progress.

It shows what part circumstance or seemingly chance occurrences may play in the forming of a career and its subsequent progress, covering all worldly affairs in a broad pattern. These, therefore, should be studied in relation to a person's own inclinations. Often, by accepting the pattern of the Fate Line, someone will pass up what seem to be

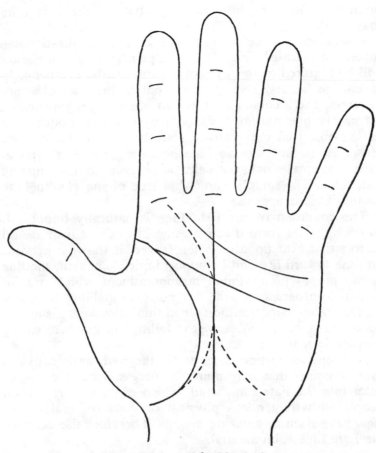

Fate Line with Variations

golden opportunities, which, when analyzed, could not have been carried through by that person.

On the contrary, a person may be curtailing his own abilities by letting himself be swayed by the factors which chance has thrown in his way. Though the pattern may be fixed, every opportunity should be seized that offers greater scope. Chance is what you make of it. That is the great point to remember while studying whatever the Fate Line may hold.

Complete absence of the Fate Line is a questionable token but not a bad one. It shows, primarily, that a person will be required to form his own career without other help or chance factors. With a strong palm, this may have advantages, and a person's career can often be prognosticated by simply placing emphasis on the strongest mounts and noting how well they can be activated by the basic lines. However, if the Fortune Line be strongly present, it will carry interpretations normally applicable to the missing Fate Line. The same is somewhat true of the Health Line should it alone appear.

The condition of the Fate Line is naturally important. In strong, clear form it activates and turns to advantage all factors that bear upon it. When frayed, it shows a nervous attitude toward life and its opportunities. Chained, the line shows moods of continual disappointment which are injurious to progress. A wide line portrays inability to recognize or follow opportunities; when thin, however, it shows a good grasp of all advantages, failing only when strong purpose is required.

A strong, deep line is naturally the best, as it activates every channel that may point to success. Health does not enter into the Fate Line at all, which explains why certain people with tremendous physical or constitutional handicaps have risen to amazing heights. Therefore the color of the Fate Line is immaterial.

Fate Lines of both hands should be studied together, for here the subjective and the objective portrayals directly strike upon heredity and environment. Birth, family traditions, and associations do much to supply the shaping courses in a person's career; yet it is through contact with the world that many chances rise and fall. Often the differences in the subjective and objective Fate Lines show where and how a person may swing from one inclination to the other, when a matter of choice is imperative. Similarly, there are times when one line is strong, the other weak, indicating a period wherein tradition or independence—one or the other—will be the route which a person may follow to best advantage.

If the Fate Line stems from the Life Line, it shows that a person will depend upon parental guidance or early training for a start in life. Often such a person continues to count upon such factors, expecting assistance from relatives or basing plans upon an expected inheritance. This will be corroborated by a large triangle at the base of the palm.

When the line begins just above the Rascette, between the areas of Venus and Luna, it fits the term "Line of Luck," because persons with such a line have the happy faculty of picking life channels to which they are best suited. They also follow a course of least resistance with surprisingly effective results. If the line actually cuts into the Rascette, it is a bad beginning, showing a penchant for getting into trouble.

Starting from the Mount of Luna, the line absorbs the imaginative and restless qualities of that area and marks the person who may try almost anything or go anywhere in search of opportunity. This is emphasized if the mount is strongly developed. Such a line is frequently interpreted to mean that some personal association, particularly marriage, will shape the career. This is a modification of the "try anything, go anywhere" motif, as it may lead to the unusual in associations.

Forks at the base of the line show that a person partakes of the varied qualities thus registered, which is usually a good token. Though it may mean early conflict, it shows the ability to shift from one pattern to another. Thus the acceptance of opportunity will not be curtailed, and one origin may prove an anchor should a person be inclined to follow an inopportune course.

Sometimes the line does not begin until some place higher on the palm. This is good, as early opportunities often lack purpose. Hence with a high start, a career that has been self-shaped until that point may enter fields that are filled with potential advantages. In any case, where the line is straight, the career will become direct and far more successful, even though personal scope is limited, than when the line is wavy or curved, representing uncertainties of purpose.

Branches reaching a high starting line near its origin naturally draw in the influences of the palm areas from which they come. The longer the branch, the greater the influence. This is true of any branches found farther up the line, all of which should be checked by the chart to learn their time period. There is something of a reciprocal effect from the line itself; it tends to activate those higher branches, pushing toward the areas to which they point. That is, there will be a personal urge toward finding certain outlets or fields of endeavor. But this depends upon the strength of the line at the periods registered.

Naturally, the palm areas must be checked to note the qualities they signify; also, their development on the palm will show how harmonious a person's own traits will be in this connection. Where a mount is undeveloped, a branch from that area will show opportunity dependent almost entirely on outside assistance.

In this connection it should be mentioned that a strong Fate Line and all its connotations may show a personal application toward bettering the opportunities of others. A married woman with a good Fate Line may think entirely in terms of her husband's welfare and thus account for his success. The same is true of partnerships, friendships, and the like, often accounting for some highly remarkable results through teamwork. Good chances can always be shared or diverted toward another person's goal. The Fate Line, throughout, is a token of human relations.

Normally, the Fate Line ends on the Mount of Saturn. The higher it goes, the better, unless it carries on to the finger, which with all lines is a self-destructive token. Ending normally on Saturn, the line activates the qualities of wisdom and sobriety, giving good judgment on all chance or opportune matters. Carrying through Saturn into Jupiter, the line shows a person who will assemble all opportunities toward some great ambition.

Should the Fate Line curve over and end on Jupiter, distinction or leadership will almost always be attained. Any branch or fork toward Jupiter points to the fulfillment of some ambition; a branch may show the time period from its connection with the Fate Line, while a fork will indicate an early pressing toward some goal.

If stopped early by the Head Line, personal obstinacy blocks the Fate Line and often thwarts a career at that point. Similarly, stoppage of the Fate Line by the Heart Line indicates that sympathy or affection will halt further opportunity. Often, however, this is a merger of Fate and Heart, shown by a join of the two lines. It means that they will carry along together toward a final goal.

Again, a comparison of the subjective and objective Fate Lines must be emphasized, now that the whole course of the Fate Line has been considered. Weakness of the subjective line—which will be covered further—will be compensated by strength of the objective, on the basis that a person can make for himself better chances than those with which he is naturally provided. When the Fate Lines are strong on the subjective but weak on the objective it shows that a person should adhere to fundamentals rather than try to cleave an individualistic path to opportunity.

Breaks in the Fate Line may come anywhere. They indicate a change in occupation, business, surroundings, or general interests. A definite break, with no overlap, shows a loss in finance or prestige, even of home; but an overlapping of the break shows a highly recuperative effect. With a long overlap, such change may be for the best. Frequent breaks, however, show too much changeability. Squares are very valuable as protective signs in all such breaks.

Small parallel lines carrying through a broken period

also will have a good effect. They show tendencies to many ventures, perhaps with a curtailment of productive ability that would seem to thwart future success. But even though opportunities be lacking at that time, the person will be placing himself in their way and often this will culminate in a newer and greater career.

Look especially for all such tokens along with peculiar conditions of the Fate Line in the space between the Lines of Head and Heart, also checking the time period so represented by the chart. This usually strikes between the ages of thirty and fifty, but will be limited to a portion of that time, according to the positions of the Head and Heart Lines. Here again comparison of the Fate Lines on both palms is most essential.

Do not mistake thin parallels along the Fate Line for islands. The parallels show a fortunate though diffused progression of the line. An island will show a loss wherever it appears, sometimes very serious. Crossed by a stray line, it traditionally signifies a love affair that will come to naught and may break up a personal career.

Crosses denote temporary failures or some sudden misfortune. A cross can be critical if it occurs at a break, and is always serious if it appears near the center of the line. At the termination, it warns against a collapse of all achievements, even a disaster to the person himself.

It must be remembered, however, that the Fate Line is a strong indicator of outside influences. When crosses barely touch it or are near it, they may not pertain to the person himself, but to someone or something associated with his interests. Often, therefore, they may not have serious effects. Oddly a square, when touching the Fate Line, may provoke bad consequences, as it can denote outside interference, however helpfully intended. Even islands have traditionally been given mystical significance, rather than regarded as tokens of some loss.

This all shows that the Fate Line, when strong, may ride over interferences. Stray crosslines or bars denote obstacles or misfortunes that are always lessened by the presence of a square; but setbacks can be expected in any pathway to success. A star at the beginning of the line is indicative of parental misfortunes; anywhere along the line it shows a danger at its charted period; at the end of the line, it warns against disaster caused by others.

In conclusion the Fate Line covers many phases of material success, but financial matters are an influence only where they are strongly pressing. What the Fate Line seeks to shape is a way of life itself, and once that pattern is aided and strengthened, commonplace problems are absorbed by it.

Long-sought ambitions, political purposes, business projects, scholarly attainments, domestic tranquility, occupational desires, and hopes of security for oneself and others all may be reflected by financial gains or losses. But with people who are content with their standard of living or who have so much money that there are no problems, the shaping of the Fate Line is every bit as evident and often more so, as their relation to life is untrammeled by financial expediency.

How we may fare in the world at getting what we most desire; the choices by which we may rise and fall; what chances may help or hinder us; who are the people most important to our lives—all those are factors of the Fate Line and whatever it represents. It is a line representing work, constant purpose, and practical application throughout life. Therein it differs from what has sometimes been called the Second Line of Fate, namely:

The Line of Fortune (Line of Apollo)   The Fortune Line, termed also the Line of Brilliance, starts from above the Rascette and carries up through the Plain of Mars into the area of Apollo. Hence it is known as the Line of Apollo, Line of the Sun, or simply the Solar Line.

When the Fate Line is absent or almost negligible, the Fortune Line replaces it, and all the data on the Fate Line

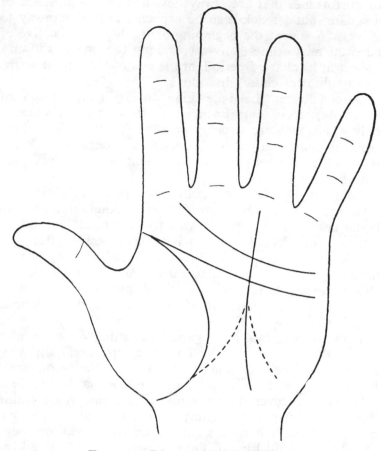

Fortune Line with Variations

should be applied to the Fortune Line, but with certain modifications. Whereas the Fate Line is termed the Line of Saturn because of its usual terminal in the Saturn area, it has a steadfast trend throughout; while the Fortune or Apollo Line, ending in the talented Apollo area, shows the application of natural brilliance to all dealings.

It will be recalled that the Fate Line occasionally runs to the Jupiter area, making ambition the ruling factor toward which a person will direct all opportunities. The Fortune Line has a similar interpretation when it stands alone. Consider it as a Fate Line swayed by an urge for fame, always through some personal skill or talent. This shows the reaction of the individual when helpful or harmful influences come into his life. He will apply all helps to increase of fame. Harm that restricts his talent will annoy him; but he will be little bothered by mundane reverses that might seem ruinous to persons of strictly worldly standards.

Complete absence of the Fortune Line has been considered a most discouraging situation, but that notion has long been obsolete. In this practical, efficient age many people can well do without it. The very term "fortune" signifies that through some skill or turn of circumstance a person can achieve a success that could not be attained through practical application. That was true during eras of conquest, discovery, and the like; but today executive ability offers larger results.

The Fortune Line now finds its fields in artistic, literary, or other intellectual outlets. It is also important in the theater, television, or wherever renown is a valuable factor. It applies to advertising, speculative finance, in fact wherever ingenuity or brilliant decisions may bring remarkable results of gain. The Fortune Line, in a word, is the jackpot of the palm.

Qualities dependent upon appearance apply to the Fortune Line as given under the Fate Line. The beginnings of the Fortune Line have modifications as follows:

Stemming from the Life Line, a dependence upon family or friends to aid the development of one's talent, or finances. Starting from between Venus and Luna, brilliant ideas that can lead to the choice of a great career, fraught with tremendous luck. From the Mount of Luna, ultra-imaginative artistry; here, practical business associations or marriage often proves the great factor toward success.

Starting from the Head Line, display of talent may be delayed, but will come from strong mental ability or genius. This is usually a talent toward finance. From the Heart Line, a sufficiency in later years, through a capable application of knowledge or abilities gained in earlier periods. These are both great strengtheners to the Line of Fate.

One peculiar type of Fortune Line starts from the Percussion in the Mount of Upper Mars and curls up to Apollo. It signifies fame and fortune through one's own efforts. Even when faint or broken, this is a very valuable line, as it denotes success despite obstacles.

Branches touching the Fortune Line apply as with the Fate Line. Tassels at the end of the line dissipate its talents. But large, wide branches extending to the Saturn and Mercury areas can constitute a triple branch with the Line of Apollo, and this is a sign of extraordinary success, often with abundant wealth.

Breaks in the Fortune Line show a scattering of talents. Here versatility can itself defeat any aim. Logically, these also show misfortunes in artistic efforts. Overlaps or squares will prove helpful, as with the Fate Line.

Other signs or markings appearing on the Fortune Line are interpreted as with the Fate Line but with two exceptions:

A star near the center of the Fortune Line may bring sudden catastrophe, but should the line be a good one, this will be offset by some great, compensating fortune.

Either a circle or a star at the termination of the line on the Mount of Apollo promises success owing to popular recognition. This is an interesting contrast to the same sign on the Fate Line, where outside influences may bring ruin. It shows how fame may prove valuable to the Fortune Line.

Where the Fortune Line serves instead of the Fate Line, the similarities are apparent. When both lines appear strongly, the Fate Line follows its usual interpretations, while the Fortune Line covers the talented phases of life. It often shows a marriage between two talented people, with the Fate Line directing home life, the Fortune Line showing one's relation to the world.

The Fortune Line should be carefully compared on both hands. Normally, the subjective line, representing natural talent, is the more important, proving that "what you have may be more important than what you may get."

Should a person constantly apply himself to new or acquired talents, the stronger the influence of the objective line.

Finally, among the triad of Destiny Lines is:

The Line of Health (Line of Mercury) Starting from above the Rascette, the Health Line sometimes stems from the Life Line; it cuts across the Plain of Mars, fringing the area of Luna, and should end upon the Mount of Mercury. It has two interpretations: one pertaining to health, the other to business. Actually it is a third Destiny Line, a substitute for those of Fate and Fortune should they be absent.

A brief consideration of the Health Line will clarify these points. When it appears, it indicates a person governed by keen discernment, hence it is often called the Line of Mercury. Like the Fortune Line, it has the functions of a Fate Line, but they are directed toward gain and rapid production.

Persons with such a line require more than usual energy to keep up with their daily affairs. When they weaken, they hurriedly try to get back into harness. Lacking the long-range purposes of ambition, wisdom, and talent, they lose their more immediate objectives if their energetic demands are halted.

Hence, in the traditional centuries when life was seldom hurried, these lapses of form were charged to ill health, partly a correct notion, since people of this type often wore themselves down. A person whose Mercury Line stems from the Life Line will always overdo things. Such a person, being independent, will not depend upon family advice or aid; thus the interpretation of family control—as applied

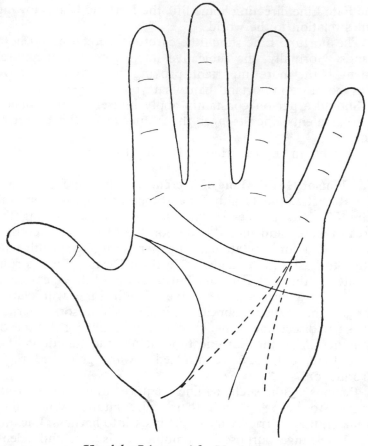

Health Line with Variations

to Fate and Fortune Lines—would not hold when the Health Line stemmed from the Life Line.

This caused the early palmists to regard the Health Line as supplementary to the Life Line, using the Health Line as an index to all ailments. Under such titles as the Line of Liver, or the Hepatica, it has been continually mis-construed. Truly it is the Line of Mercury, and might today be properly termed the Business Line. But we shall retain the title of the Health Line because a person actually does need to be healthy to shape his destiny through its findings.

Complete absence of the Health Line is excellent. It in no way restricts any discernment which a person may possess from a well-developed Mount of Mercury. Such qualities may be activated by any other line. When it does appear, the Health Line activates the quality of discernment to the exclusion of many others if the line be strong and well formed. Where it is found faint or barely traceable, it shows fitful efforts by the person to use discernment or business talent as a wedge where other attributes fail.

The Health Line should be clear and preferably deep. It is a good line if thin, because it should not have too strong a color. When wide, it shows a person apt to overtax himself; noticeably red or yellow in color, such a line has been said to denote fever turns and bilious attacks respectively.

Frayed, the Line shows nervous qualities that hamper efforts; chained, it indicates sluggish and depressive moods which account in part for the old-time health interpretations.

Stemming from the Life Line, it shows a strong inheritance of physical traits and business acumen, but often discloses a feverish urge toward independent accomplishment. From near the Rascette between Venus and Luna it shows more originality in everyday affairs. Starting from the Mount of Luna, a person will have what seems a true intuition toward all commercial enterprises, depending on the development of the Luna area. Forks at the start usually show a conflict of these forces.

When the Health Line begins higher on the palm or comes in strongly at some charted point, it shows a sudden turn to enterprise at that period. The Health Line should be straight; when wavy or curved, it shows an unpredictable, often envious trend in business matters.

Branches usually extend toward Apollo and are a very good token. They show distinct improvements, often expansion in purposes wherever they are charted. When the Health Line ends at the Head Line or the Heart Line, it shows activity in business or daily work. Here the Health Line checks with the same time period on the Life Line, marking the cause of any unfavorable effects registered there.

Success in work, profession, or business is heralded by the Health Line that carries clear to the Mount of Mercury. If it shows forks there or is tasseled, it indicates a decline in later activity. A fork over to Apollo is excellent. It marks a clever person who is often talented as well.

Breaks in the line indicate successive business reverses often owing to an incompetence which the person will blame on poor health. When the breaks overlap, there is quick recuperation from such losses. A person whose Health Line shows such breaks should make a thorough study of both palms to determine his most important and strongest qualities, since his natural business urge is sufficient to carry him through his problems if he has chosen a suitable field. Squares, of course, protect against these breaks.

Islands are very serious signs with this line. They show failure of energy and therefore check again with the Life Line. All other signs check closely with the Fate Line, bearing similar interpretations, but applied far more to work, professional, and general business problems. Hence these signs can be interpreted by referring to those under the Fate Line, remembering that the Health Line sometimes entirely replaces it when the Fate Line is faint or absent.

When the Fate Line is missing but the Fortune and Health Lines are both strongly present, they are the equivalent of the Fate Line and divide its functions. One, however, is almost sure to be stronger, and should be given preference. In this class, for example, are persons who have both artistic talent and business discernment yet who often make the wrong choice, losing from one what they might have gained from the other.

A triangle of which the Health Line forms a component part and which appears upon the Mount of Mercury is a sign of rare genius, usually of a scientific nature. A star at the end of the line, on the Mount of Mercury, indicates some extraordinary achievement.

In comparing the palms, the subjective Health Line is the key to inherent weaknesses. It shows possible lapses in physical energy, the periods when a person is most prone to ailments. Otherwise, the objective Health Line is the more important. Particularly with an energetic person, the objective signs show what may develop. It can record business reverses as well as illnesses. Often it shows problems or misfortunes which a person is likely to bring upon himself.

In both cases all signs should be tallied with the same period of the corresponding Life Line. Though specific health interpretations are largely obsolete, any obstructed energy of the Health Line may show its result upon the Life Line, indicating how serious the consequences may prove.

Among other secondary lines is one called:

The Cephalic Line Known also as the *Via Lascivia* and the Milky Way, the Cephalic Line is a short but often well-defined parallel to the Health Line. It can be considered a sister line to the Health Line, which it sometimes strengthens. If only one line appears in this area of the palm, it is regarded as a Health Line.

The Cephalic Line, when it occurs, is found near the start of the Health Line, farther over on the Mount of Luna, toward the Percussion. When straight and well formed, it is a fine adjunct to the Health Line if the hand is a strong one with a fairly firm palm and if the Mount of Luna is not overdeveloped.

Under such good auspices the Cephalic Line, as far as it goes, adds to the energetic qualities of the Health Line, often giving a person the ability to conduct two enterprises at once. The Cephalic Line also strengthens any Health

Line deficiencies, and the longer it is, the better, unless it crosses the Health Line, which will denote a conflict of interests.

However, when wavy or with a curve toward Upper Mars, the Cephalic Line indicates excesses and dissipation, even extreme sensuality, when the palm lacks strong traits or shows bad indications of its own. All surplus energy may then be put into riotous and intemperate living with wasteful expenditures. A star on the line signifies riches that will be squandered as rapidly as gained, if other indications are bad. Breaks and other features are defined as with the Health Line.

Often persons with the strongest and most successful Health Line have the Cephalic Line also. This may account for the extravagances and sheer abandon that often accompany big business sessions. Also identified with the Health Line we have

The Line of Intuition (The Line of Luna)   Aptly styled the Line of the Moon, the Intuition Line begins in the Luna area, near the Percussion, and normally follows an inward curve that continues as a crescent, going outward through the Mercury area until it again nears the Percussion.

An opposite twin of the Cephalic Line, which represents the utter in the physical realm, the Intuition Line goes equally far into the mental limbo. Indeed persons who regard palmistry as an occult science class the Intuition Line as purely psychic. Certainly people who have such a line are the great hunch players. Some analysts, therefore, have classed the Intuition Line as a variant of the Health Line attributed with immense business foresight. This is far from the case, for a strong Intuition Line often diverts its owner from any practical application of his peculiar gift.

Exceptionally strong when found on the subjective hand, the Intuition Line shows a person who strongly favors presentiments and will often be guided by them. The higher the line starts on the Mount of Luna, the stronger this conviction, often as a result of personal experience. A person with this line ending upon the Mount of Upper Mars will often show a pronounced interest and ability in hypnotism.

Branches, which are usually not much more than frays, show a nervous and often irritable disposition, which stirs the restless Luna nature in small ways. Breaks show spasmodic intuition which may often go wrong. Islands often indicate somnambulism. Found on the objective palm, the Intuition Line shows a person who believes in the psychic and will often develop intuitive qualities, since all the listed traits are present but slower to operate. On both palms the psychic quality may become a dominating force.

A rare but highly interesting variant is the Reverse Line of Intuition wherein the crescent faces outward toward the Percussion instead of inward. Though they believe in anything from hunches to full-fledged premonitions, people with the reversed line are almost entirely wrong on every chance they play. In fact, their uncanny ability to miss on so many things is an equally strong proof of the strange sway which the Intuition Line holds over those on whose palms it appears.

The Line of Mars   This is a sister line to the Line of Life, curving within it, closer around the base of the Thumb. It gains its name from the fact that when fully formed it begins on the Mount of Lower Mars, thus acquiring some of its forceful strength. It is a very fortunate line, even though it be fragmentary, for whatever strength it has is added to that of the Life Line.

The Line of Mars never appears alone, for if it did, it would be regarded as the Life Line. When it covers only a short curve, its strengthening influence is limited to that period as charted on the Life Line. Sometimes, however, it continues on beyond a short Life Line and then is valuable indeed, as it carries the vigor of the personality that much further.

Through a close, even microscopic examination of the Hand traces of the Line of Mars may often be discovered and prove a slight but nevertheless effective adjunct to the Life Line, often helping to counteract unfavorable signs on that line. If the Line of Mars, well formed, has bad signs or markings, they should be interpreted as with the Life Line; but if the Life Line itself is strong at that particular period, any such signs will be subordinated.

The only fault with the Line of Mars is when it is too strong, as it may add too much activity to the Life Line, much as the Cephalic Line can act upon the Health Line. Coming from Lower Mars, it brings aggression, sometimes resulting in a violent and highly intemperate nature.

One distinctive and highly favorable sign that may appear, especially upon the Line of Mars, is a star, which is interpreted as recording a deed of extraordinary bravery.

CHAPTER 13

THE LESSER LINES

The lesser lines are those which appear on many palms. They have been studied sufficiently to allow accurate and special interpretations. They are usually shorter than the basic and secondary lines described in the two previous chapters and are often found in restricted or fragmentary form. In almost every instance, however, they are highly active and sometimes take on great importance. This applies quite frequently to

The Girdle of Venus This line describes an arc or downward crescent from between the Fingers of Jupiter and Saturn through the Mounts of Saturn and Apollo, rising up to a point between the Fingers of Apollo and Mercury.

The Girdle of Venus is a sensual line, sometimes denoting an ungovernable temper as well as passions. When found in complete form, as a single line, it is almost a sister line to the Heart Line, which it strengthens. In turn, the Heart Line may be a controlling force over the sensual activity represented by the Girdle of Venus. Often this activity will find its outlet through artistic efforts or channels.

Should the Girdle be double, the sensual factor is increased and is all the more difficult to control. When the

153

Girdle is triple, any excursions into debauchery or license—as indicated by the double formation—are apt to become an outright policy. Nevertheless, there can still be controlling influences found throughout the palm. Where the higher mounts are well developed, the basic lines strong and highly activated in purposeful directions, the indications of the Girdle are subordinated by more powerful tendencies. But should the palm already show considerable inclinations toward sensuality, the Girdle of Venus may become its chief controller.

When the Girdle shows a wider span, terminating on the Mount of Mercury, much of its sensual force will be expended in nothing more than high nervous energy, provided the palm itself is a good one. When the Girdle is deep, cutting through such lines as those of Fate and Fortune, depraved tendencies will injure a promising career. Should the Girdle be thin, with either of those same lines cleaving it, a strong palm will rule over sensuality.

When the Girdle is only faintly traceable, its domination is accordingly less, and will show itself in the excitement of nervous spells, sometimes leading to hysteria. Broken lines composing the Girdle may make sensuality more marked, but they also denote the nervous or hysterical side. This is because an incomplete Girdle indicates a retiring trend in contrast to the bold, profligate manner that the full arc stimulates.

Often the Girdle shows terminals but no center curve. These are strong indications of its sensual sway, but, as with very faint markings, caution can show control. Also, to be highly active, the Girdle should be strong on both palms, as either natural or acquired caution is apt to restrain the abandon of the other factor.

Lines or bars cutting the Girdle of Venus are bad signs, showing fits of hysteria or extreme excesses that may be ruinous to a person's fortunes. A star on a strongly formed Girdle is also a very bad sign.

The Ring of Solomon   This is a slightly curved line which girds the Mount of Jupiter. In full form, it starts from between the Fingers of Jupiter and Saturn, curving downward toward the side of the palm to a point above the beginning of the Head Line. Even when only partial, it signifies a nature fond of the mysterious. When large and strongly formed, the further will a person plunge into the lore of the psychic or occult. This line is corroborated by a marking called the Mystic Cross, mentioned in the chapter on signs.

The Ring of Saturn   This line forms a mark like a ring just under the Saturn Finger. Its name has been erroneously applied to the Girdle of Venus with which it has no connection and for which it should never be mistaken. Though one end of the Ring of Saturn starts between the Fingers of Jupiter and Saturn, it stays so close to the Saturn Finger that it is easily identified.

The Ring of Saturn typifies a person who is lacking in definite purpose, often changing moods as well as occupations, rarely for anything but worse. It is common, therefore, upon palms of unsuccessful persons. Its fault is that it segregates the Saturn Finger from the mount, thereby preventing the Fate Line from activating the finger.

When broken, the Ring loses some of its troublesome indications, as the finger gains thereby. Sometimes, instead of an actual ring, there is a cross which has the same effect but can be even worse, as it also has the significance of a Cross upon the Saturn Mount, described in the chapter on signs.

Lines of Affection   More commonly termed the Lines of Marriage, these are also called the Lines of Union. As Lines of Affection, they are better named, as they do not always signify marriage. Rather, they indicate a companionship, often resulting in a period of engagement which may be broken. Too, they indicate other close family ties of marital origin.

These lines start on the Percussion or outside of the palm, just below the Finger of Mercury. They come in toward the palm and enter the Mercury area in a straight line. Sometimes there is only one; but there may be two, three, or even many more. Each represents an affection, and its length determines its importance. Usually they terminate as they reach the Mercury area, but they may extend much farther.

A straight line is the best, often signifying a good marriage. A forked line indicates a separation, but not through the fault of the person on whose hand it appears. If a line turns up, its owner reputedly will die first; if it turns down, that rule will apply to the companion. Dots and stars have the latter interpretation also.

Only the most prominent of these lines signify marriages; others merely represent strong affections. Where two lines run so close together that they appear to be a double line, this is a "Mother-in-law Line," indicating that some member of a family—often but not always a mother-in-law—will live with a married couple or be very close to them.

A broken line indicates a separation, which may mean divorce. If the breaks overlap, a reconciliation is signified. Long separation or divorce is indicated when an extremely long Affection Line slants or branches clear down across the palm, cutting the Fortune and Fate Lines. It causes trouble and loss with each line that it crosses, including the Life Line, if the slanted Affection Line continues through to the Mount of Venus.

A straight Line of Affection stopping short of the Fortune Line (on Apollo) is a good sign, indicating a brilliant marriage. Should it cut through, misfortune will result. An island on an Affection Line is interpreted as an intrigue; many islands, more intrigues. If there are vertical lines on the Percussion, through which Affection Lines run, those verticals traditionally signify children from a marriage, but this is pure conjecture.

Lines of Opposition Similar to the Affection Lines are others that come from the Percussion on to the Mount of Upper Mars instead of Mercury. They represent opposition on the part of other people, though the person who has such lines may generally invite it. This is because the lines activate Upper Mars with its qualities of resistance and desire for justice.

If short, the Opposition Lines mean petty or inconsequential matters. As they lengthen, they can indicate actual antagonisms and lawsuits. Often one of these markings will develop into a long line, which will run straight across the palm or downward, cutting through various important lines and even carrying through the Life Line.

An Opposition Line can therefore threaten fame, mind, honor, or family, as represented by the Lines of Fortune, Head, Fate, and Life respectively, always through legal complications, as this is definitely a strong lawsuit line. Whether or not the person will win out is unpredictable; but in any event he will become deeply involved. This special line may often be found on the palms of judges, attorneys, or others connected with the law; sometimes on palms of members of their families.

If this line curves upward, it may cross the Line of the Heart and reach the Fortune Line, in which case it represents legal problems concerning the affections. The exception is found when the Fortune Line is otherwise absent and this line from Upper Mars replaces it. In that case, instead of an Opposition Line, it becomes a special form of the Fortune Line, as described under that head. It shows an ability to achieve fame and fortune through one's own efforts.

Lines of Travel These are lines coming from the Percussion into the Mount of Luna and also include some lines that slant upward on the mount itself. Traditionally, the lines on the Percussion, mostly horizontals, indicated voyages by sea; those on the mount, journeys by land. This is an obsolete interpretation, but there is little doubt that these lines signify a travel urge.

Lines on the Percussion follow that interpretation and therefore also indicate a restless, frequently nervous disposition. When numerous and crossed by stray lines, they show that a person is subject to fatigue, either mental or physical.

Oblique Travel Lines have more significance, especially when the Mount of Luna is highly developed. Starting from near the Rascettes, they show great possibility of travel, the amount depending on the length and number of lines. Should they reach any basic or secondary lines, they will press the travel urge upon such lines. The same applies to Travel Lines starting higher in the Lunar area when sharply formed, particularly at their origin.

These must not be mistaken for branches coming from the basic and secondary lines, which dwindle as they enter the Lunar area. With such, a line itself actuates the area.

Sometimes a strong, well-defined line from Luna will carry as far as the areas of Jupiter, Saturn, or Apollo, and thus form an auxiliary Fate Line. It should be studied along with the Destiny Lines and given similar interpretations, remembering that its Luna origin gives it imaginative and restless activity. Also, its goal will be the terminal area which it activates.

Lines of Influence   Light, short lines that radiate from the Venus area and carry through the Life Line, going just beyond it, are termed Rays of Influence, and merely signify disturbances in a person's mode of living at the periods where they show such crossings.

There are stronger Influence Lines that start from the Mount of Venus, within the circle of the Life Line. They differ from branches which fade toward their terminals after leaving a general line; for these Lines of Influence are most sharply defined at their starting points in Venus. Should such an Influence Line stop where it meets a general line, it shows an outside influence that affects the person. Reaching the Fate Line, it might mean a marriage or a liaison. Reaching the Fortune Line, it could show another person influencing one's career. Similar interpretations are given to meeting points on other important lines.

The great difference between an Influence Line from Venus and a branch going from a general line to that area is that the force comes from someone else instead of emanating from oneself. Usually the influential force is represented by someone within the family circle or a close friend of long acquaintance. Marriage, of course, is included in the family sphere. The Venus influence has already been discussed with the Affection Lines.

Where a strong Influence Line carries to another mount we find the outside force operating therein. For example: An Influence Line from Venus to the Mount of Jupiter would show some other person aiding one's ambition, and so on, according to the interpretations of the mounts. The development of the other mount is helpful here, for then the Influence Line may aid it. But where the mount is absent, poorly developed, or even overdeveloped, the Influence Line may show a nagging, goading policy on the part of family or friends without beneficial results. Often, however, the wishes of the goader will be gratified.

Study such lines carefully, because sometimes they are more sharply defined on the other mount instead of Venus. In this case, the influence is reversed. It shows the person who can use his family, relatives, and friends to further his own purposes.

The Line of Escape often can be classed as a secondary line, as it appears quite strongly on some palms. This has been termed the Escape Line, and it forms a sharp connecting line between Venus and Luna, running across the bottom of the palm. If it starts deeper and more sharply in the Venus area, it shows a person so annoyed by problems coming from family or career that he will seek some form of escape.

This may be through wandering, drink, or other indulgences. Many women with this line often become great eaters. Condition of the Escape Line, such as frays and double or triple formations, augments this condition. Signs and markings are significant and follow common interpretations. When deeper and sharper on Luna, it shows people whose very restlessness will cause them to become escapists, even though provocation is slight.

Sometimes the Escape Line can be slightly traced through a series of short stray lines. They are evidence of this special Influence Line, indicating that it will show its force sooner or later.

The Lines of Family Within the circle of the Life Line are curved lines, often faint, that have often been termed Influence Lines confined solely to the Venus area. Considerable studies have been made of these, but they are only supplementary to the usual palm analysis. Being within the life circle as represented by the Life Line, they symbolize the family. Following the course of the Line of Mars, they acquire the added strength attributed to that line.

In fact, these Family Lines are practically identical with the faint form of the Line of Mars, as described under its head. Since the Line of Mars, when faint, lacks strength to bear upon outside matters, it would naturally show an influence in the province wherein a person is normally at home; namely, the family.

So interpreted, these lines represent various friends and relatives who will influence a person's life during different periods, often in the form of lasting impressions after a loved one is gone. On the subjective palm such lines show an early, almost hereditary influence of family. On the objective palm they show a later turn to family and friends, often the forming of a family of one's own.

The stronger the marking, the more the influence of these lines upon a person's life, and sometimes they are very sharply etched. (See chart, page 104.)

The Rascettes On the wrist, just below the base of the palm, are girding horizontal lines often termed Bracelets. They may total from one to five in number, sometimes crossing or running into one another. As with the Life Line, age probabilities were once computed by these lines, each representing approximately twenty-five years, but this traditional notion has long been obsolete.

The only important Rascette is the top one. Clear, well defined, it promises a life free from too much struggle. When frayed, chained, close to the palm, or actually upon it, the Rascette signifies that hard work will be necessary to achieve success. Struggles may continue, often demanding long, continued effort until late in life.

When the Rascette touches any general lines, it influences them. This is helpful only when the Rascette is perfectly formed. Otherwise it is harmful, as any irregularities in the Rascette become restricting influences and promise difficulties. These are transcribed in terms of the line so affected. (See chart, page 104.)

The Thumb Chain This is the vertical line that runs straight downward at the bottom of the second phalange of the thumb, dividing the thumb from the Mount of Venus. Sometimes, instead of being a well-defined single line, this is a linked chain, or consists of overlapping segments giving that effect.

Such a chain is a token of an argumentative disposition, indicating people who are especially fond of getting in the last word. (See chart, page 104.)

CHAPTER 14

SPECIAL SIGNS AND MARKINGS

One of the most interesting phases of palmistry is the identification and interpretation of odd markings which appear in various areas or on the lines. Some of these— crosses, squares, grilles, and the like—have already been described and analyzed in part but will be detailed further in this chapter. First, however, we shall consider more conspicuous formations, beginning with

The Quadrangle This is the space between the Lines of Head and Heart, which represents two of its sides. The other boundaries are imaginary, being considered as the limits of the Mounts of Jupiter and Upper Mars. The space between the Head and the Heart Lines represents the balance between mental and emotional activities. Therefore, should the space be unusually wide, it shows that the mind lacks control over the desires, thereby indicating a person who will want his own way regardless of consequences.

Should the lines come quite close together, head controls heart, revealing a self-centered personality. Further interpretations of the Quadrangle are superfluous, as it is covered under the Plain of Mars, but it contains special markings that will be mentioned. Next in order comes

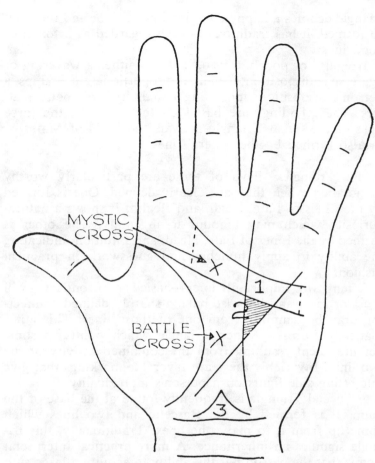

1—Quadrangle; 2—Great Triangle (Shaded Area—Minor Triangle); 3—Special Triangle

The Great Triangle Composed of the Lines of Life, Head, and Health, this figure is seldom completely formed, but its boundaries are considered as if closed at all angles. When large and with its three component lines clearly traced, this triangle denotes a happy combination of vigor and intellect; so formed, it has traditionally been regarded as a token of good luck.

Irregular or poorly traced, it shows either a wavering or aggressive disposition; small, it proportionately cramps a person's disposition, indicating irritability over petty 'matters. These findings are based on the fact that the three lines of the Great Triangle activate the Plain of Mars.

Also formed by the general lines are

Minor Triangles Two of these are particularly worthy of notation when they are clearly defined. One is formed by the Lines of Fate, Head, and Health. It shows a natural curiosity which may amount to ingenuity. The other is formed by the Lines of Fate, Head, and Intuition, indicating the ability to apply hunches and guesswork in practical fashion.

Often two important lines—basic or secondary—will cross or meet and likewise have a sharply defined connecting branch stemming from one of those lines. This automatically forms a Minor Triangle which points to some definite talent resulting from the combined activity of the two lines. Invariably these are favorable markings that give interesting side lights on a person's individuality.

A Special Triangle is frequently found at the base of the palm. It is formed by the Rascette and two lines which come up from it to make the apex. Traditionally, this triangle signifies an inheritance. A more practical interpretation is that the person has the ability to acquire a large sum of money through a stroke of genius or good fortune and is very likely to do so. (See Fate Line.)

Other Triangles All triangles are favorable signs wherever they appear. Touching any of the basic or secondary lines, they point to helpful conditions or occurrences at the time represented. Also, they aid in activating the line. Often they can be tied in with significant events in a person's career, hence this should be carefully checked with a person's past and studied in terms of future potential. Specific interpretations have been given to triangles appearing on certain lines, but as a rule their application differs according to individuals.

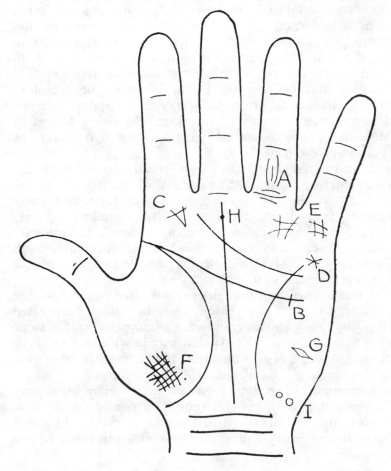

A—Stray Lines; B—Bar; C—Triangle; D—Star; E— Squares; F—Grille; G—Island; H—Dot; I—Circles

Independent triangles found on the mounts add to the qualities of those areas. In very rare instances they appear on the fingers and have the same effect. These triangles are usually quite small, whether on mounts or fingers, but are very important, being tokens of high abilities or qualities.

On the Mount of Jupiter, a triangle designates a diplomat or mass leader; on Saturn, it shows power of concentration or study in a chosen field; on Apollo it indicates ability to blend scientific methods and artistic efforts, often with financial success; on Mercury, it shows executive ability in business and politics; on Luna, it shows opportunities through imagination or travel; on Venus, happiness or distinction through family or marriage. On either Mount of Mars the triangle betokens high honor through bravery or special achievement.

All such triangle indications are greatly dependent on the fuller interpretations of the palm. What the triangles represent are possibilities, and sometimes they relate to matters of comparatively short duration. Where mounts are only slightly developed, the presence of a triangle indicates favorable results from outside sources rather than through one's own individual efforts. This has led to the triangle being interpreted as a very lucky sign.

These independent triangles are not often found upon the mounts, which is one reason why they have been rated so highly. They cannot counteract a bad palm, and in some such cases triangles have typified people with extraordinary cunning instead of fine qualities. But in most instances triangles should be considered as of high account.

Sometimes when found on the lines, triangles occupy portions of crosses, but still should be considered as good tokens, either tempering bad fortune or producing something favorable to counteract the bad significance of the cross.

Crosses   Crosses denote obstacles or interference whenever they touch a line; their interpretations have been detailed in chapters covering the general lines. Similarly, they generally have a serious influence upon the mounts when they appear there. On Jupiter, a cross offers a good significance, that of a great affection or a happy union, but it is sometimes a token of infidelity.

On Saturn the cross is a fatalistic sign; on Apollo, it means thwarted fame; on Mercury, it indicates evaded issues or bad dealings; on Luna, self-deception; on Venus, family quarrels; on either Mount of Mars, violence or danger from enemies.

Similar interpretations are given to crosses that appear upon fingers or thumb, but fortunately the obstacles indicated by crosses may prove to be petty rather than important. This shows personal tendencies to turn small issues into large, often with disastrous results. Isolated crosses found in the Plain of Mars, for instance, are indicative of unwarranted outbursts of temper, often causing trouble with family and friends.

This applies particularly to a large cross found in the center of the Great Triangle, which is traditionally known as the Cross of Battle. In contrast there is the Mystic Cross which is also large and appears near the center of the quadrangle. It shows a love of the mysterious and is regarded as a companion sign to the Ring of Solomon, the two showing a nature much intrigued by psychic or occult subjects. The Mystic Cross, which may be partially formed by a general line, is considered a favorable sign.

Stars A star is usually a highly fortunate sign. It differs from a cross in that it has one or more additional points or bars. These must be formed by stray lines; hence a cross appearing on a general line should never be mistaken for a star. A star promises high accomplishment in most instances, but also indicates considerable intensity, which is its one danger.

On the Life Line, a star is doubtful. It may mark some brilliant event, but possibly with serious repercussions or a severe shock. On the Head Line, a star shows overintensity with maddening results, particularly if the star appears at the termination of the line. On other primary or secondary lines the very intensity represented by a star promises high success in whatever those lines indicate.

The same applies to stars found on the mounts with one exception: that of Saturn. On all the other mounts a star gives promise of success, honor, or celebrity through the particular quality represented by the mount. Simply intensify the readings of those mounts, signal out the achievement that seems most plausible, and the star will become the indicator of a desired result. With Saturn, however, the very association of intensity with the melancholy of that area may class the star as a mark of tragedy.

Any isolated stars on the Plain of Mars also have unfortunate but often brief significance. They are symbols of bad news pertaining to family or friends; they also deter a person from achieving certain desires. Though long regarded as a purely traditional interpretation, this rule holds with remarkable accuracy.

Squares and Grilles   Squares are the great protective signs and have been discussed in connection with the mounts and lines. On the mounts they offset any unfavorable markings found there. On the lines, they mend breaks, nullify bad signs, and generally aid in the activation of an otherwise weak line. Rectangles are a companion form of square; these figures may be irregularly formed but are still considered potent, even though one of the four sides may not be quite closed. No side of a square or rectangle, however, can be formed by a general line.

Grilles, which are formed by crisscrossed stray lines producing a screen effect, have been summed up in connection with the mounts. They detract from the qualities represented by any mount on which they appear and bring out the bad traits of those areas.

Other Markings Islands have a serious effect upon lines on which they appear, as detailed in chapters covering general lines. Sometimes islands are found on stray lines located on the mounts. In such cases they weaken the qualities of those mounts.

Dots have been mentioned with the general lines, whereon their significance is bad. When they appear on mounts, they accentuate any bad sign already there.

Circles indicate defects, often of a physical nature, on any line where they may appear. Found on a mount, a circle may be disregarded except on the Mount of Apollo. There it is a very fine sign, accentuating talents of the individual.

All markings, when found on thumb or fingers, can be taken as applicable to the mounts closest to those members, although they have traditional interpretations of their own. This is also the case with

Vertical and Horizontal Lines Such lines have been analyzed quite thoroughly among the special features of the mounts, the general rule being that verticals add to the development of the mount but show uncertainty or scattering of effort if numerous.

The exceptions are strong verticals on Apollo or Mercury. On Apollo, they are termed the Lines of Reputation, often in conjunction with the Fortune Line, and form a highly favorable sign. On Mercury, they represent the Medical Stigmata, showing an urge toward medicine.

Horizontal lines detract from the mounts in most instances, and the same is applicable to some diagonal lines. The important cases have been covered with the mounts, as having a particular bearing on them.

When vertical or horizontal lines appear very strongly upon thumb or fingers, they should be given the general interpretations. Verticals add to the quality of the nearest mount, except when numerous. Horizontals show failings or weakness in the traits of the mount.

With these lines, however, interpretations may be gauged in terms of the phalanges on which they appear. With the thumb, the first phalange denotes will power; the second, reason. The fingers have the interpretations of intellectual, practical, and material, representing the three phalanges in order. Thus such lines show in which realm strength or weakness may be found.

So many meanings could be given to lines and other markings found on the thumb and fingers that they would constitute a minor study in themselves. But that very term —minor—applies to their significance in comparison with the greater and much more accurate findings of the palm. Hence the traditional variants of thumb and finger markings do not come within the range of general palm analysis beyond the scope already given.

Final Notes on Markings   In the study of markings, which includes all frays and other peculiarities of the general lines, the use of a magnifying glass greatly facilitates the analysis. Though much can be learned by ordinary survey under strong light, the glass brings out and clarifies all the tinier formations, aiding greatly in their proper identification.

Use of the glass, along with a slight compression of the palm, will reveal many features which might otherwise escape notice. Often it is thus possible to trace the courses of general lines among the numerous markings and contours which form the fascinating map of life.

CHAPTER 15

A COMPLETE PALM ANALYSIS

Note: This analysis is based upon a study of a pair of actual hands, which are illustrated in detail on pages 172 and 173. The left hand in this case is the subjective, the right the objective hand. In the preliminary survey, the hands are treated as one, as they are similar in general formation. As differences become more apparent, they will be treated under the subjective and objective classifications.

This hand is of the mixed type, but shows two conical and two spatulate fingers, indicating inspiration and energy along with adaptability. In a preliminary survey (not depicted) the hand proves to be pliable, indicating talent, though hampered by circumstance. Soft consistency shows a changeable nature; the thumb approaching the right angle adds an unmanageable factor.

On all fingers the first joints are smooth, the second joints knotted. Ideas will be spontaneous where all traits are concerned, but analysis will be shown in practical matters. Wide nails (not depicted) show an outspoken person; fluted, the same nails show a nervous disposition.

In length, the fingers are close to normal, but being slightly on the short side will show some impatience over detail. This is accentuated by the long first phalanges, showing consistently intellectual desires.

171

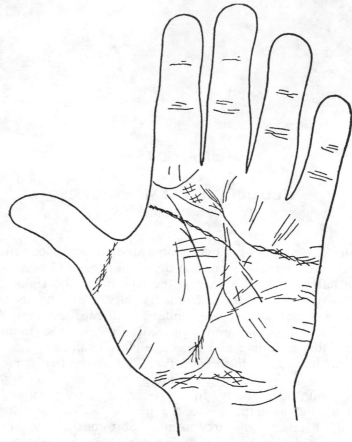

Specimen Palm—Left Hand (Subjective)

Low set, the thumb shows a careless, overgenerous nature. Of average length, it is suited to the conical and spatulate types. The second phalange being longer than the first indicates a mind that rationalizes everything, stronger on logic than will power. Of normal width, the thumb shows a straightforward nature. It has a flat first phalange, show-

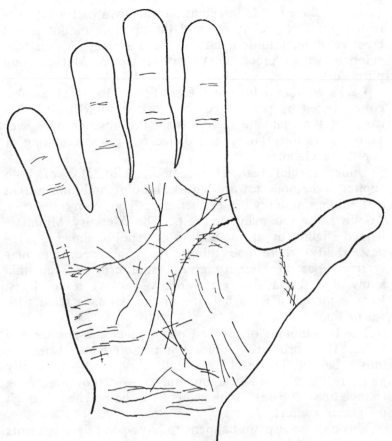

Specimen Palm—Right Hand (Objective)

ing a nervous energy that must be expended to avoid irritability.

Among the developed mounts are Jupiter, showing ambition with pride in artistry and perhaps unrecognized talent, because of the conical finger. Apollo, with finger of spatulate type, shows artistic originality and versatility.

Luna developed adds imagination and love of travel; controlled by a conical finger and thumb, this mount shows creative urge, intuition, and nervous energy. Venus, developed, shows practical sympathy; Upper Mars, strong purpose.

Lacks on this palm are the studious Mount of Saturn, compensated by preference for work over sociability because of the spatulate finger. Also, the absence of Lower Mars shows uncertainty, avoidance of issues, shunning of popular acclaim.

Under special features we find inclinations of both Jupiter and Apollo toward Saturn, holding ambition in rein and adding stability to exuberance. Too many lines on Apollo show too many interests. The Mercury Mount is helped slightly by an inclination of Apollo, showing business ability where fine things are concerned. Irregular vertical lines on Mercury give a smattering of scientific knowledge. Luna shows too many restless travel lines; Venus, though a good balance to the palm, is filled with worry lines.

The two mounts of greatest prominence are Jupiter and Luna. They ordinarily indicate a person who wishes for things beyond his reach, but with this hand—its knotty joints restraining practical impetuosity—it shows a strong chance of such gains. Achievement can be reached through imaginative effort.

This particular palm happens to have good developments of Apollo and Venus as a secondary pair. Combining sympathy with artistry, this blend is weakened by the low-set thumb, indicating a rule of personal whims. However, the combination furthers the promise of the Jupiter and Luna realm.

Summed up to this point, the hand and palm show:

A natural inspiration is furthered by both talent and imagination. Spontaneous ideas and unusual nervous energy stimulate a creative urge, which, in turn, is drawn by ambition. Though careless, restless, and often uncertain, this person has purpose and exuberance, which are sufficiently stabilized to promise great accomplishment.

Failure to recognize one's own talent is a bad factor, teamed with avoidance of issues. But the natural, practical sympathy, combined with artistry, plus a desire for work, should more than compensate for this. Control of impetuous desires is a fine point, and this person should avoid too much detail and too many interests.

Against such a background, which tallies rather closely when the subjective and objective palms are compared, we come to a survey of the lines.

Fairly high at its starting point, the Line of Life adds energy to natural ambition. Chained, it shows a nervous and probably delicate childhood. It strengthens as it proceeds, with a warning of diminishing forces from frays— or downward branches—appearing in later years. The line shows a remarkable extension, signifying that with care a ripe old age should be reached.

A branch coming from Jupiter signifies tremendous ambition influencing the Life Line. There are no serious obstructions other than interference lines, which could mean imaginary problems instead of real ones. This branch appears to be a portion of the Life Line, extending through the Head Line, but a careful study of this particular palm shows that the branch lacks the sharpness of a basic line.

On the objective hand, the Life Line conforms fairly well with the subjective, except for certain signs. In the early years, a succession of tiny triangles show that natural imagination was being developed and forming a tremendous impression. Upward branches show spurts of new interests, becoming stronger and more vital. Crosses show danger, or warnings of it. Two large crosses show toward the age period of the fifties, but they form triangles as well. The first might signify a marriage. The triangles could mean some inventive triumph, the crosses being a precarious factor.

The Line of Head on the subjective palm begins with

the Life Line, showing natural caution, with a possible fear complex or backwardness in early years. Chained, this line shows uncertainty in decisions and lacks fixation of ideas. These both activate the adverse qualities of the palm, but the Head Line improves as it continues. Apparently interferences before the age of thirty-five serve to strengthen the mental capacity of the line. Two extensions of this line show a double talent.

A comparison of the objective palm shows a large separation between the Head Line and the Life Line. This represents the development of a reckless streak. It confirms the nervous impetuosity of the first phalange of the thumb. It has a strong branch coming from Jupiter, showing the mind's development toward ambition. This tallies with the double extension on the subjective line. The objective line has only a single extension, but it is strong and drops very low on Luna. This shows that the owner should follow the talent that deals with an imaginative or creative field.

Starting high on Saturn, the Line of Heart shows a sensual nature, tempered by good judgment, which, however, is weakened by the presence of many branches. Though free from breaks, the line has an island (under Apollo), warning against overstrain. This often shows in eye trouble. Frayed and tasseled at the end, the Heart Line shows a weakening like the Life Line. Strain must be avoided in later years.

Crosses with an island (under Mercury) signify ill health with financial loss. This calls for comparison with the objective palm. There, the Heart Line lacks such adverse tokens, hence heeded warning can avert misfortune. On the objective palm, the Heart Line starts from between Saturn and Apollo. This shows that affection will be attracted by brilliance, more so as the years progress.

The Fate Lines (subjective and objective) should be compared throughout. The subjective stems from the Life Line, showing acceptance of family guidance through youth. The objective, rising from Luna, shows planning, during those early years, toward interests far removed from the family sphere. A triangle on the objective line indicates an intense, inventive faculty in this direction.

The subjective Fate Line shows crosslines, representing serious obstacles or sharp changes. Three of these appear between the ages of thirty and fifty and represent domestic problems, perhaps divorce or serious business problems disturbing domestic tranquility. These are corroborated by the objective palm showing similar crosslines. During this critical period the subjective Fate Line is practically a broken line, though with good overlapping, producing thin parallels.

This shows many ventures and changes but at no time failure. Crosses in the Plain of Mars show mental pressure and fear complex probably active at this period. However, the objective Fate Line is unbroken during this period, indicating that the person can maintain a single path. Along with it is a light parallel signifying a subordinate and probably helpful interest. Most vital is the square (about where the Fate Line reaches the Heart Line). This is the saving factor and turning point in this person's career.

For, though the subjective Fate Line shows varied interests persisting from then on, the objective Fate Line sharply portrays single purpose, which should become the person's logical choice.

A study of the Fortune Lines tallies with this. On both palms the Fortune Line starts late, above the Heart Line. This means sufficiency in later life through early acquired ability. The double Fortune Line in the subjective palm promises a dual talént, but the line on the objective palm indicates a strong major purpose with an accompanying minor interest.

Thus the Fortune Line substantiates the Fate Line, and the best advice would be to follow the strong purpose that they show.

On both palms the Health Line is only lightly traced and therefore of minor importance. It shows fitful periods of strain, because of illness, worry, or business uncertainty. Some of its early breaks tally with childhood illnesses indicated on the Life Line, but otherwise the Health Line discloses no strong or serious tokens.

Other secondary lines are lacking on these palms.

Among lesser lines, the subjective palm has the Ring of Solomon, indicating great interest in the occult and mysterious. This is corroborated by a Mystic Cross, irregularly formed and not too strong, because it involves a general line (the Fate Line).

However, on the objective palm there is also a Ring of Solomon, showing that the person will follow this natural bent. It is corroborated by a fine, independent Mystic Cross which makes this reading highly positive.

The single Line of Affection on the subjective palm indicates marriage. The area itself, being very developed though not marked, gives possibility of one or more marriages. The objective palm shows three such lines, two crossed by a bar, meaning sudden termination of affection, thus fitting with the first reading.

Each palm shows Lines of Opposition. One on the subjective palm is long though broken. It shows a tendency to lawsuits. The others are "enemy lines," representing personal antagonisms or petty quarrels. They are comparatively few and slight as palms go.

Both palms show a fair quota of Travel Lines. These are mostly short, appearing on the Percussion, those on the objective palm being more numerous. They show a restless nature and many short journeys. The oblique lines crossing Luna on the subjective palm appear to be branches of the Fate Line, giving it imagination. All lines of this sort are open to varied or dual interpretation. Lack of oblique lines on the objective palm foreshadow the lessening of imaginative qualities.

The palms show many Rays of Influence, but only a few reach the Line of Life and those are in the early years, showing nervous disturbances during that period. This tallies with the thumb formation and the restlessness of Luna.

On the objective palm, an Escape Line is apparent in a fairly clear but irregular form. This would show that at intervals this person will seek escape from pressure or problems by whatever means is most convenient. This may be attributed to the obstacles and fears shown by the crosses on the subjective palm.

Influence of friends and relatives is shown on the subjective palm by the Lines of Family, but, though numerous, these are very light and not too important. The Rascette, running high and showing slight chain formation (on both palms), defines the person who will work hard and long for success and will prefer activity. The Thumb Chain, with its argumentative trend, may account for some of the obstacles traceable in these palms.

The Quadrangle is somewhat cramped, showing a self-centered personality but in a studious way, coming under Saturn; but with the Saturn Finger of spatulate type and therefore energetic, this carries its force along the descending Head Line, which extends far into the Lunar area. This, plus the presence of the Mystic Cross, concentrates all activity upon imaginative work and therefore is a powerful factor in this person's life.

The Great Triangle, a trifle cramped and irregular, shows a slight irritability on the subjective palm. Wider, with better lines on the objective palm, it shows a developed vigor and intellect. The Special Triangle (found on both palms) shows unusual good fortune, fitting well with the interpretations of the Fate Line. Certainly the ability is present to acquire large sums of money, as the Special Triangle would indicate.

Most of the other signs have been covered so far, with the exception of a few reserved for special discussion. These are the squares appearing on the Mount of Jupiter, on the subjective palm. With Jupiter supplying this palm with high ambition, the squares are a great protective element against errors by the individual. Their absence from the Jupiter Mount of the objective palm would indicate that the individual had improved his prospects through the years.

Also, on the subjective palm, the Mount of Jupiter is crossed by an unusual line, which activates Saturn as well, since it extends into that area. A slighter line, higher on the mount, would show interference with ambition. But this line is too strong, too well defined, to be anything other than an asset.

At passing glance it would seem a branch of the Heart Line, coming from the Jupiter area, but close observation shows that it does not connect. That leaves only one conclusion: since this line runs parallel to the Head Line, it should be identified as a second Head Line, which is very rare, but quite evident in this case.

This corroborates the findings of the parallel Fate Lines, the same peculiarity with the Fortune Lines, also the double quality of the Ring of Solomon and the Mystic Cross. The Fingers of Saturn and Apollo are the only spatulates on the hand; they represent the energy expended in the fields of Fate and Fortune. In fact, this palm tells a double story, which in itself justifies the conclusion of the double Head Line.

The added Head Line is needed to fulfill the attributes of the palm. Without it, the whole analysis would be unbalanced. The guiding influence needed for the carrying on of alternating careers—as is indicated by the palm reading —is supplied by the second Head Line. This is why the objective palm shows an attained balance over the colorful but somewhat unruly subjective palm.

You will find many other remarkable instances in your study of palms, all leading to discoveries of your own, which will come as the surprising result of confirmed conclusions. From these you will gain a greater, deeper understanding not only of palmistry itself, but of the people whose characters disclose themselves through the interpretations of scientific palm analysis.

INDEX

181